The Counselling Interview

A Guide for the Helping Professions

Helen Cameron

First published in 2008 by
PALGRAVE MACMILLAN
Houndmills, Basingstoke, Hampshire RG21 6XS and
175 Fifth Avenue, New York, N.Y. 10010
Companies and representatives throughout the world.

PALGRAVE MACMILLAN is the global academic imprint of the Palgrave Macmillan division of St. Martin's Press, LLC and of Palgrave Macmillan Ltd. Macmillan® is a registered trademark in the United States, United Kingdom and other countries. Palgrave is a registered trademark in the European Union and other countries.

ISBN-13: 978–1–4039–4727–7
ISBN-10: 1–4039–4727–9

This book is printed on paper suitable for recycling and made from fully managed and sustained forest sources. Logging, pulping and manufacturing processes are expected to conform to the environmental regulations of the country of origin.

A catalogue record for this book is available from the British Library.

A catalog record for this book is available from the Library of Congress.

10 9 8 7 6 5 4 3 2 1
17 16 15 14 13 12 11 10 09 08

Printed in China

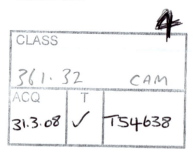

Contents

Introduction

This book focuses on the skills and processes used by a range of helping practitioners to interact with clients to explore the nature of their situations and concerns. The process of conducting interviews is central to the work of many of those employed in most social care settings and so this features in education programs preparing students for such work.

Commonly applied communication processes enable practitioners to intervene at key points where people interact with their environments and this is often through competently managed interviewing. This interviewing work includes a variety of assessment and intervention services at primary, secondary and tertiary community and health care levels with individuals, families and a range of community groups. It occurs in all these areas, whether formally organized or occurring naturalistically within aspects of work. Face to face and head to head then, practitioners listen, respond and creatively work with all sorts of people in supporting their search for a better life.

The purpose of this book

The primary purpose of this book is to support the development of readers' knowledge and skill in conducting human service interviews, in particular in managing the process with intentionality and empathy. A well-managed professional interview achieves its purposes whilst also attending to the care of the individual client. In this sense this book is also about doing no harm. It also adopts a strengths-focused approach in many respects. The book is intended to be of value to all those who plan to work as helpers – as social workers, nurses and a range of others in the human services.

Who is the interviewer?

The interviewer referred to throughout this book is the person in charge of a helping interaction and who sees their role as assisting the person

I

who is usually their client, to explore life issues and to understand their own contribution to their problems and to locate solutions that work for them in a long-term sense. The helping professions – social work, health and welfare work and community work, to include just a few fields of endeavour – comprise an essential field of practice in most countries. Practitioners interact with clients across the full range of health, family, youth, justice, housing and education service sectors in most societies. Such workers are located in the full scope of human services – in federal, state and local government settings, in non-government organizations and in other public and private providers. For example, the International Federation of Social Workers (2000) defines social work broadly as a profession that promotes social change, problem solving in human relationships and the empowerment and liberation of people to enhance well-being, utilizing theories of human behaviour and social systems. The skills and processes discussed in this book are basic to ethical professional practice and assist readers consistently to apply competence and care in this important work.

Throughout the book at times the terms interviewer, counsellor, practitioner, worker and helper are used interchangeably to refer to the person conducting a 'helping' interaction. In the title and throughout his book, Hugman (2005) refers to most of these professional groups as 'caring professions', defined as those undertaking 'work in which the human person is both the object and subject whether physically, mentally, emotionally or spiritually' (Hugman 2005, p. 1). It is the case then that social workers, health workers and others employed in the human services frequently sit down with their clients and begin a conversation to find out what is happening in their lives and work with them to locate possible solutions.

The helping model in this book

The model of helping described in this book is reflected over several chapters and is based on strengths-focused work and on a three-stage process. In the *first stage*, clients are encouraged by the interviewer to focus on their situation to locate the matters most in need of attention. This is generally referred to as a process of *exploration* where clients are encouraged to think more clearly about their feelings, the situations surrounding them and what they are doing to cope with it all. This first stage segues into the *next stage* which focuses more clearly on *the behavioural goals of clients* – both in terms of coping behaviours (for which clients are affirmed and which are the foundation for later work) and sometimes in terms of dysfunctional behaviours that complicate their lives and may need to be changed. The *final stage* is about locating a *stepped* and carefully arranged *change process* that supports clients to build on and learn additional coping strategies and to locate solutions. Essential features of this model include a *strengths focus* where all clients are affirmed as experts in their own lives in terms of current coping capacities (De Jong and Berg 2008, p. 18) and a *cognitive-behavioural approach* in reference to the consistent focus on behaviours in all stages and the goals and change processes employed in supporting clients to learn new life skills.

Qualities of the effective professional helper

As helping can occur in a wide range of settings, are there some stable practitioner skills and competencies that are effective in most settings? I believe so and these are detailed throughout several of the following chapters. For example, competent practitioners know how to *begin interviews*, to *focus them* on relevant issues and *to conclude* them. Effective helpers also employ *culturally appropriate nonverbal skills* and *verbal responses* that show respect for and understanding of their clients. The *verbal skills, as* discussed in Chapters 2 and 3, are primarily reflective and empathic in nature and focus on clients' *feelings*, the *situations* they are currently in and their *behaviour* within these. This is also achieved with the use of *purposeful* and *deliberate* focusing skills where the practitioner guides the client to begin the interaction, to discuss and move between productive issues and to conclude with a sense of achievement. A successful interviewer then is *actively empathic*, productive in terms of *achieving outcomes* and focused on clients' *positive coping skills* and ultimately on *solutions*. Competence is also about *values* and the ability to accept a wide range of cultural perspectives in clients' life management issues. Finally, *self-care* is important as effective helpers understand the erosive potential of emotional labour and have lifelong strategies to support themselves physically, cognitively and emotionally.

Using this book

It is recommended that each chapter is completed in sequence as this will allow reading, reflection and any related practice activities to be approached with a background of previous understanding. Ideally, the guidance of a tutor or teacher will assist readers in interpreting the meaning of it, in structuring practice activities to illustrate and demonstrate issues and skills and in providing feedback on skill progress and knowledge development. For readers studying without such guidance, I hope this book provides perspectives on the counselling interview that are relevant to each reader's specific learning needs.

The book begins with a description of basic skills and processes involved in the helping interview, the three stages of the helping process and current contexts of human service work. Then it examines the process involved in initiating the helping interaction and moves on to paraphrasing – a major response type in the empathic enterprise. Questions and other probes are described as part of managing the direction and focus of the interview. The book then moves on to goals and action work and the use of techniques related to motivational and cognitive-behavioural approaches. Helping when crises occur, including violence and self-harm, is discussed and the book concludes with a discussion of stress, self-care and reflexive qualities in managing the important work of interviewing in the human services.

CHAPTER I

Overview of Processes, Stages and Contexts of Helping

This chapter provides an overview of skills and processes needed to competently manage a *single* interview, such as referred to in the range of settings discussed in the introduction. By interview, I mean a professional interaction entailing a dialogue between helper and client as may occur in a range of settings. Such interviews may focus on gathering some basic information about the client, making an initial assessment of their ability to profit from further work together and then engaging them in a range of processes appropriate for their needs. Following this, features of a *staged* process are described. The latter two stages may only be appropriate where more long-term work with clients is possible although some aspects may be employed in many professional interactions. Some of the contexts of human service work in current society are complex and entail a range of challenging variables for many practitioners. Clients and practitioners in the twenty-first century are faced with a range of confronting contextual pressures – some personal and social in nature including value-based matters and some organizational. The gender of the helper and the client is also important. These contexts provide a foundation to the further descriptions of skills and processes in the following chapters of the book.

Processes and stages within the single interview

The qualities and skills discussed in this section refer primarily to the competent management of a *single* interview, perhaps the first or only one. Most of the skills and processes referred to briefly in the following overview, however, are important aspects of any well-conducted interview at all stages and for whatever purpose and so have broader application.

Beginning the interview effectively

First impressions are important. Making this first contact a positive experience for a client entails managing a range of processes with care and courtesy. These first processes are often described as 'meeting, greeting and seating' the client, where the client and interviewer meet, exchange greetings and maybe some brief small talk and settle into seats. Once seated, the interviewer attends physically and psychologically as described by Egan (2007, pp. 74–78), briefly introduces self, explains the overall purpose of the interview if this is known in advance and mentions how long the interview might need to be. The practitioner identifies any issues concerning confidentiality and/or professional obligations to disclose if these are relevant at this point. Finally, the client is asked what they hope to achieve in this interview if it turns out to be worth their effort in attending and then the client is invited to begin their narrative.

Responding with a range of reflective and empathic responses

Responding refers to both nonverbal and verbal behaviour showing attention to and understanding key aspects of a client's narrative. Clients focus on situations, including perceptions about other's behaviours, their own reactions and behaviours and their feelings. The effective practitioner responds empathically, deliberately and purposefully to this range of aspects. Cormier and Nurius (2003, p. 65) describe empathy as 'the ability to understand people from their frame of reference rather than your own'. Empathy is also the active demonstration of this understanding of the clients' feelings and perceptions *through verbal responding*. To me empathy is not just an abstract cognitive process – although it may well start there – but a verbal demonstration of understanding. The most meaningful response – the paraphrase – where reflection of clients' feelings, situations and behavioural aspects demonstrates understanding of each and then causally links these in a verbalized response, provides the most empathic response. The helper's ability to focus clearly on these different aspects – feelings, situation and behaviour of the client – establishes a foundation for goal-focused work in due course. As well, the skill of summarizing provides an empathic overview of key points of the client's achievements in the interview. Responding, although primarily focused on the client's frame of reference, may at times re-frame what the client says, by emphasizing positive behaviours or by focusing on some aspects rather than others, although not at the expense of accuracy and empathy. At all times, the professional interviewer aims for a presence that is active, empathic, focused, genuine and interpersonally warm.

Managing direction and movement throughout the interview

The effective interviewer is responsible for facilitating the direction and flow of the interview. This entails assessing when sufficient range and depth of information on an issue has been gathered and then supporting the client in making a shift of focus – or transition. This begins with a summary of the issue under discussion and a declaration of intention to shift the topic. This shift is managed through the use of an open probe that invites information from the client and invites them to focus on the next issue. It is important to follow the client's disclosure on this new topic with empathic responses and not with further questioning. The ability to combine empathic responding and clear focus is a key feature of helper competence.

Achieving the work of the interview

The work of the interview is what happens between the beginning and the conclusions and depends on a number of factors such as whether it is a first or consequent interview. As well, the communication skills and focusing abilities of the client may be a factor. Most interviews have a purpose, and achieving this is largely up to the practitioner who needs to keep the client productively focused if possible whilst also maintaining an empathic approach. This requires a balance between the interviewer's empathic reflective functions and the active direction of the interview's focus. As the interview develops, this may include focusing on goals and clients' behaviour change. A goal and action focus does not mean talking about big scary leaps towards change. Focusing on *small first steps*, combined with appropriate focus on positive client attributes, is reassuring to clients who feel overwhelmed by life problems.

Managing the conclusion of the interview

This final phase entails its own set of challenges. First, it requires a clear signal of the intention to finish the interview, to prepare the client for this. Next, it is important to summarize the key achievements of the interview and facilitate some client evaluation of its success. Finally by affirming the client for their achievements during the interview and agreeing on further contact if this is appropriate, the interaction moves firmly and respectfully towards its conclusion.

Key points on processes and stages within the single interview

➤ First contact colours a client's feelings towards the interviewer, the interview process and the nature of further work together

➤ Nonverbal attending, reflections and paraphrases, with a positive focus when appropriate, are essential aspects of empathic responding

➤ Managing change in the focus of the interview is an essential hallmark of the competent interviewer

➤ Managing the work of the interview requires a balance between directing the focus according to the stage of work together and being empathically responsive to the client

➤ Effective conclusions place key aspects of the interview centre stage and establish a positive basis for any future contact

---

Stages in the helping process over several interviews

In much of the literature about interviewing and counselling, most writers refer to *stages* in working over time with clients (Ivey and Ivey 2003, Egan 2007, De Jong and Berg 2008, Miller and Rollnick 2002, Young 1998, Hutchins and Vaught 1997, Okun and Kantrowitz 2008). Usually two or three major stages are described by various writers. In this book, the first stage is described as one of exploration where issues are considered, the second is one where the client gains deeper understanding about their current behaviours and starts to formulate goals or areas for work. The final stage focuses on the client achieving and evaluating these goals and consolidating these new skills into their life.

Some practitioners in the human services field may be lucky enough to work in settings where they have sufficient time to work with clients on enough occasions to support them through this kind of life change process. I recognize, however, that the work of many in the field entails shorter sessions and limited occasions for substantive contact with clients. Work with many clients then takes place under time pressure and it becomes difficult to guide any longer-term change process. When this is a common feature of practitioners' work, then shorter sessions and less of these – maybe only one – may mean that only some processes are achieved or that the stages are concertinaed into a much briefer period.

If time is too limited to consider a staged change-focused process, a very brief session managed courteously and empathically may have a positive impact and leave the door open for further contact in the future. Okun and Kantrowitz (2008, pp. 261–262) describe the success of 'brief therapy' when it is 'direct, active and present/future oriented' and is based on a positive relationship between helper and client. Evaluation of outcomes from brief therapy by De Jong and Berg (2008, pp. 235–240) indicates that this brought positive outcomes within around 3–5 sessions for the majority of clients in the study. Hutchins and Vaught (1997, p. 59) mention a study indicating that 78 per cent of clients said they felt much better following a single session only. It is important to consider at this point that helping is always for better or worse and is never neutral as suggested years ago by Carkhuff (1977, p. 2). How well we relate to a person and respond to them empathically in terms of their immediate needs, feelings and goals impacts on how that person feels about the practitioner, the helping process, herself and her future.

The following material describes these stages in more detail, emphasizing the skills and processes that contribute to the conduct of effective interviews, whatever the stage and setting for the work. Attention to empathic responding remains a central aspect of all interviews at all stages.

Stage one – making a connection, exploring issues and gathering relevant information

Any text in the area of interviewing will provide some focus on the importance of the first stage, where connections are forged between worker and client. Ivey and Ivey (2003) refer to a range of skills and behaviours used in connecting with clients, sometimes referred to as establishing rapport. Other well-known authors in the field emphasize the importance of these initial skills and processes of the first phase of an interview. Egan (2007), De Jong and Berg (2008), Okun and Kantrowitz (2008), Cormier and Nurius (2003), Miller and Rollnick (2002), Corey and Corey (1999) and Brammer and MacDonald (1999) all include a similar range of verbal and nonverbal behaviours that establish an attentive environment for the client to begin to narrate their story. During this first stage, if client strengths are identified fully, a beginning focus on how things could change may emerge.

Stage two – locating client strengths, directions and goals

In stage two, the worker begins to use techniques and processes that stretch or extend the client's immediate view of self and their situation, to encourage deeper self-understanding and self-appreciation of own strengths. Affirmation may further strengthen client self-esteem and support the client in generating goal-directed thinking. De Jong and Berg (2008, pp. 75–79) also stress that this process is really about amplifying what the client wants, rather than the worker suggesting completely new ideas. Stage two interventions assist clients to understand what they are managing well and how to build on these skills to achieve the changes they see as needed. The worker needs now to combine empathic responding skills with positive goal-focused talk. In goal-directed work, responses are used to focus less on deficits and more on 'complimenting client strengths and successes' (De Jong and Berg 2008, p. 248).

Stage three – action strategies for change

Interventions in stage three are about helping clients to use solution-focused plans to make real changes in their own behaviour to achieve what they want in life. Such interventions encourage the client to make firm decisions about their life circumstances and how to change these for the better. In stage three, clients are helped to make clear plans of action and implement these to change life circumstances through their own efforts. Anything that works to mobilize the client is worth considering, so long as a good foundation of trust and understanding exists between client and worker.

It is essential to encourage clients to take small steps to move towards change. Okun and Kantrowitz (2008, p. 168) and Hutchins and

Vaught (1997) classify issues, goals and interventions under three main headings – affective, cognitive and behavioural. McGuire (2000 [a] and [b]) suggests the use of cognitive-behavioural therapy or CBT. This book favours a cognitive-behavioural approach, once a basis of trust and clear view of issues has been established, with emphasis on clear behaviourally focused goals. A full exposition of this approach to change is really beyond the scope of this text. A much fuller discussion of this range of change strategies is described in Cormier and Nurius (2003), Simos (2002), Barlow (2001), Ellis (1998), Beck (1997) and Beck (1995), all of which may be useful to practitioners interested in helping clients to work towards achieving productive change in their lives.

So far, this book has examined some issues related to the basic processes and stages of human service interviewing. Now it moves on to look at some of the contexts surrounding current professional practice within human services work that render the ability of the practitioner to be competent, flexible and self-aware all the more important.

The contexts of modern interviewing practice in the human services

There is a range of personal, social and cultural contexts for current interviewing practice in the twenty-first century that impacts on many aspects of practitioners' work with clients. These contexts include shifts in perceptions about standards for social behaviour and ideals in current society. Gender frames also impact on the processes of an interview, as do values and organizational imperatives for efficiency and effectiveness in some fields.

Personal and social contexts for modern life

The social and cultural conditions of the last century produced a range of problem-focused counselling theories and set up conditions that have shaped the modern 'self' of clients – and of counsellors too. Giddens (1991, p. 74) suggests that the pre-modern individual, in the centuries preceding the last, was more passive and less reflexive and consequently less troubled by ideals of personal, psychological perfection. But as Hunt (1999, pp. 20–27) says, self-regulation is not a recent thing and social ideals have been an important aspect of human existence for centuries, although issues have shifted. The focus of moral "correctness" has varied, of course, from century to century, ranging over aspects of social and personal behaviour, including manners, public presentation guidelines, religious observances, work, gender roles and sexuality, gambling, and uses of alcohol and other mind-altering substances such as opium. Some of these remain issues for modern existence, even if perhaps the drugs have changed and religious observance has been reincarnated as concerns about Sunday trading (Hunt 1999, p. 20). Focus on psychological or mental health ideals has strengthened in the last century, becoming much more intense for the individual. As described by Hunt (1999), the twentieth century saw a shift from a concern for moral character, as in the previous centuries, to a fascination with personality, or 'personal self-formation through self-discovery and with the "work" of forming a distinctive individual identity' (Hunt 1999, p. 4). These modern images, promoted in a number of ways through a range of agencies, universalize ideal frames of personhood that are largely Euro-American in origin. Rose (1998, p. 25) refers to the 'regimes of the person', ideals implanted in the institutions of Western societies, which have worked their ways into many features of individuals' thinking. This leads people to engage in conscious positioning of self, a process filled with risk and uncertainty for the modern individual.

Today in the twenty-first century, individuals are likely to invest much more time (and money too), in trying to maintain and improve their personal image and many continue to worry intensely about whether they measure up to current ideals – physically, psychologically and socially. People stare at images of other men and women on TV and in magazines and worry about being able to attain the desired standards of personal appearances, the body beautiful, perfect family, big house and smart car – and other trappings of cool success. The landmines of gender roles, relationships and lifestyles have existed for centuries but need to be negotiated more carefully now by everyone – young and old. If individuals "fail" in that they cannot attain these personal and social ideals and have problems in their families and other relationships, then self-esteem plummets and they feel like outcasts in society, unaware that many others are secretly scrabbling to try to reach these same standards of perfection.

As the caring professions grew out of modernist projections about a perfect society, the formulation of agreed standards for how to live one's life may be promoted by professionals thus engendering non-acceptance of diversity and difference. Current work in the human services, however, faces many with a range of clients' lifestyles, ethnicities and beliefs. In part, the ability to maintain an accepting pattern of responding is underpinned by the practitioner's awareness of self, rejection of unrealistic social ideals and the ability to approach all interactions with interest in the uniqueness of every client.

Shifts in human consciousness during the twentieth century have also been characterized by the emergence of what Rose (1998, p. 75) calls 'technologies of subjectivity' as reflected in psychoanalysis, existentialism, behaviourism, gestalt therapy, rational emotive therapy, reality therapy and so on – many of which have been adopted by helping professions such as social work and psychology. In Ellul's 1965 analysis of what he terms the technological society (in Woolfolk 1998, pp. 30, 31), he suggests the focus of helping professions became one of providing solutions to individuals who do not have a problem. More insidiously perhaps, many of these theoretical ideals found expression in newspapers and popular magazines, in conversations in pubs and restaurants, at the dinner table and between parents and children. Terms such as *defensiveness, mid-life crisis, acting out, resistance, psychological games* and many other notions from psychology, psychotherapy and psychiatry are all to be heard in social conversation.

The focus of psychology, social work, psychotherapy and most other 'caring professions' (Hugman 2005, p. 1) thus became one of 'correcting' clients with a range of perceived *disorders, dysfunctions* and *deficits* they may not have had before encountering the practitioner. *Problem solving* on behalf of clients, seen as dysfunctional or lacking in some way, became the hallmark of professional expertise. Unfortunately, many clients still presume this is what counsellors, social workers and the like are supposed to do – to be the expert. These socializing, regulating and deficit-based perspectives became imbedded in many mainstream approaches in human service work. Much of this is a fruitless exercise as people cannot be (should not be) forced to change. Jamrozik (2005, pp. 330, 331) suggests, despite the proliferation of human services, 'The professions working in these services, not withstanding their good intentions, have done very little for the people they profess to serve'. Rose (1998, p. 75) suggests the helping professions have used processes that render clients complicit in naming psychological ideals and related dysfunctions and then in struggling towards ideals of health defined by expert others. Low self–esteem thus has become the burden of the individual in consumerist, modern societies and the challenge now is to help clients to unpack these modern pressures without buying into their negative self-esteem by focusing on standards of perfection in psychological health.

Values contexts in professional practice in the human services

Anyone who believes they can operate from a *value neutral* perspective is deeply mistaken. Personal and professional values influence every aspect of behaviour. To add further complexity, some clients have been socialized to expect a kind of 'problem-solving paradigm' to operate in their dealings with interviewers. This may mean that many clients approach the interview expecting to be told what is wrong with them and how to fix it, as suggested by De Jong and Berg (2008, pp. 6–7) thus opening themselves up to value-based advice about possible solutions. Rose (1998, p. 98) takes it deeper and describes processes whereby individuals become complicit in shaping and regulating their own person based on these professional ideals.

During a professional interview where there is close interpersonal communication, it is therefore easy to encumber clients with the practitioner's values and beliefs about their own lived experiences. This may come across as injunctions about how clients should behave, producing a range of reactions in them from compliance and relief, in dependent clients wishing for strong direction, to existential anxiety or plummeting self-esteem for those who are less sure of the expertise of the worker. Potter (1996, p. 121) notes, however, that values operate as *undeclared* evaluations and judgements about other people and their behaviours and practices and may not be easily detected by some clients. Clients from the dominant mainstream culture may have better defences against value-based judgements from the interviewer, but when clients are from a different culture, they may be deeply puzzled and confused about behavioural or cognitive ideals conveyed (sometimes quite subtly) by the practitioner. Understanding how the interviewer's own beliefs impinge on clients during a professional interaction involves deconstructing idealized views of the person and understanding one's own professional and personal values and knowledge.

Payne (1997, p. 4) points out that the practice basis of social welfare, for instance, has traditionally been an ethno-centric one (Anglo-American) and as such may not apply to non-Western societies, or to current Western pluralities. The professional interview can become instrumental in a situation where 'those who happen to find themselves in positions of power are able to determine ... what knowledge is to count as relevant' (Howe 1994, p. 526). This underlines the importance of interrogating professional values and their fit within the diversity of current society.

This interrogation is not always simply achieved. It may be that a practitioner's professional values honour client self-determination, autonomy and empowerment, whereas in their actual behaviour, the interviewer responds with premature advice and low empathy, viewing the client as dependent and resistant. On the other hand they may act in accordance with their professional values but these values may be at odds with those who come from cultural groups that value obedience to moral, social or religious rules over individual rights and freedoms.

The world of values and ethics is complicated and complex. Hugman (2005) provides a carefully considered analysis of many issues related to this troubled field in current practice in what he calls the 'caring professions'. It is clearly important for practitioners in all settings to understand their own values about people and to be responsible for maintaining ethical and culturally competent frames of professional practice. In part this is about being fully aware of the influence of own professional, cultural, religious and social heritages and when required being able to rise above these influences to work in a culturally sensitive and competent way. Gudykunst and Kim (1997, p. 254) refer to 'establishing a psychological link' between own cultural beliefs and those of the other person. They see this as a hallmark of effective interaction with others. They suggest this 'culturally transcendent' perspective, as they term it, has the potential to overcome some of the pressures inherent in negotiating diverse cultures in interviewing.

Fortunately I believe a harmonic of cultural sensitivity has become somewhat stronger in recent decades and many writers in the interviewing field include this theme in their texts. Several are concerned to redefine practice away from cultural hegemony. There is strong support for culturally sensitive practice as in Bankart (1997); Ivey and Ivey (2008); De Jong and Berg (2008) and Corey, Corey and Callahan (2007). Several authors have renamed skills and processes too, in recognition that names are powerful containers of perceptions and experience. I believe this renaming also reflects a tectonic shift in professional values. So, in some recent editions of texts, *counselling* becomes, or is at least accompanied by, the more neutral *interviewing*. Counselling can imply the presence of expert frames, even when the approach is client centred. The terms *therapy* and *problem solving* are replaced by the more positive and client focused *problem-management* (Egan 2007), or *solution building* (De Jong and Berg, 2008). The focus has changed to one of working alongside clients as they identify and build on their strengths (Saleebey 1997; Ivey and Ivey 2003) and of recognizing clients as experts in their own lives (De Jong and Berg 2008). A fairly broad consensus on these issues has recently developed and this is reflected in many new editions from the established writers in the interviewing area. I interpret these shifts as strong signs that the tacit belief in the goals and processes of traditional deficit-focused approaches has faded.

A *strengths perspective*, with a focus on coping goals, is particularly well suited for application in a broad range of interviewing work, especially where clients are struggling to come to terms with change. Interviewing with a client struggling to cope with family upheaval, employment loss, or change in health status calls for approaches that focus positively to affirm the person's skills and capacities and to build or rebuild their self-esteem. The experience of loss – of personal capacity or of work roles, for instance – and the sense of hopelessness that clients feel in the face of such loss call for approaches that help people to efficiently relocate their strengths, rebuild self-esteem and regain control over their lives. The reconstruction of a positive self-image through the revision of self-talk, emphasis on coping skills and other positive goal-focused approaches employing small steps towards change, such as in Cognitive-Behavioural Therapy (CBT) and motivational approaches, are now seen as instrumental in effective intervention. These ideas feature strongly in the work of key writers in the field, such as De Jong and Berg (2008), Ivey and Ivey (2008), Egan (2007) and Miller and Rollnick (2002) and in further chapters of this book.

Organizational contexts of human service work

In many areas of practice within organizations providing human services, there has also been a less positive shift from a broad social justice perspective in human service provision, to a stronger and more unashamedly open declaration of the need for greater economic efficiency in service delivery. Okun and Kantrowitz (2008, p. 4) note the move in current work towards 'primarily short-term, outcome-oriented' practices. This is reflected in an increased emphasis on 'outputs' and on heightened efficiency in client services. As well, expectations are placed on many clients to cooperate psychologically and economically in their own and their family members' care. The tenets of economic rationalism, together with the influences of now long-standing managerialism, and recent 'user-pays' models subordinate other principles and values previously seen as a basis for the provision of welfare services in Western society. Many agencies, pressured by economic-rationalist government policies, are providing fewer resources but are demanding greater efficiency from human service workers. This is described as happening by a range of authors, for instance, in Australia by Alston and McKinnon (2001, pp. xxiii and xxiv), in the UK by Davis and Garrett (2004, p. 21) and in the USA by Neukrug (2004, p. 294).

Predictably then, there is also acknowledgement in the interviewing literature – for instance, in De Jong and Berg (2008), Coale (1998), Egan (2007) and Okun and Kantrowitz (2008) – of the need to accommodate organizational pressures to achieve increased accountability and efficiency in interviewing. In particular, De Jong and Berg (2008) have articulated the case for an approach to practice that is both briefer and more focused on achieving client outcomes. Fortunately there is some intersection of concern here. Effective and brief work has an attraction for agencies (hell-bent on doing more with less – and quickly!), but it also has appeal for ethical practitioners who like to achieve positive and efficient outcomes and for clients desiring value for their financial and/or personal investment. However, economic rationalism also means many clients may receive less support from human services than was available in the past. Okun and Kantrowitz (2008, p. 4) suggest briefer approaches may well suit some, such as the 'worried well', but may not match the needs of those seeking support for chronic physical and mental health matters.

The enterprise movement can be viewed as the basis of an organizational context that has re-defined the meaning of human service work. It is aimed at 'achieving employees' normative commitment to a politico-economic order in which the values of the market-place dominate all other moral values (Legge 1995, p. 85). Such a perspective has seriously eroded the continuation of expected financial bases of welfare provision in society and has starkly challenged the values of traditional social work which has certainly been subject to down-sizing, out-sourcing, contractualism, competition and cost cutting.

According to Howe (1994, p. 528) legal relationships are replacing 'therapeutic alliances', and social services are becoming increasingly characterized by 'contractual arrangements, service provisions and social rights'. In the field of social welfare, contractualism fits poorly with the traditional expectations of both client and worker. Many of the areas of welfare provision intersect with aspects of personhood which are imbued with little sense of choice for either client or worker, such as intransigent illness or disability, unemployment and poverty.

Traditional practice approaches may appear threatened in the rational-economic frames within which practice occurs. Professional interviewing is enacted within workers' obligations and accountability towards employers, and many practitioners will need to negotiate conflicts of interest between personal, professional and organizational principles. Sacco says the dominant culture is 'materialistic, liberal-capitalist' and 'utilitarian' among other things and 'is researched through a stated or implied literary-based discourse' (Sacco 1996, p. 33). If this is the case, then the traditional moral framework for many human service workers is at odds with our pluralist, multicultural society.

O'Connor et al. (1995, p. 48) consider one of the major tasks of social welfare workers is to mediate the effects of the residual welfare state in its function as provider (or outsourcer) of social support in a number of directions. Currently this may require them to act as gatekeeper, to interpret the welfare system and to respond to the unintended negative effects of the rationalization of services. The work of the social welfare practitioner, already subject to internal dissonance, now also includes the need to explain the effects of economic rationalism on their already underprivileged clients. Jones and May (1992, p. 12) stress the need for a heightened awareness of these powerful and sometimes negative effects of departmental policies on the clients they are also committed to help. It is a difficult task, however, to explain to a client why there are fewer funds, less access to supports and longer waiting lists for services, for instance, when their disabled child's needs remain just as urgent.

To add further complexity, Jones and May (1992) and Camilleri (1996) suggest that much of the organizational work of human service professionals is not very visible or well supported. Jones and May (1992, p. 276) note that 'human service workers often stress the confidentiality of their relations with consumers' as do many other professional groups such as clergy, doctors and lawyers. The tension between confidentiality and duty to warn or report is another common pressure.

Camilleri reveals the personal and private nature of much of human service practice through his discussions with social workers about their work. He stresses how private and invisible is the world of the social worker (Camilleri 1996, p. 201). This is reflected in Aldridge's comments about Johnson's (1972) idea that 'professions like social work have considerable operating space as a result of their guaranteed flow of clients and the privacy of the professional encounter' (Aldridge 1996, p. 185). Harrison (1991, p. 79) makes the point that the processes of working in the human services 'are dictated in part by the agency, the law, the clients, and in part they are developed in the minds of social workers in action'. Freidson (1986, p. 162), in referring to teachers' work, calls them 'brokers between policies established from above and the concrete conduct of the classroom' and this idea is even more applicable to a broad range of current human service work where client contact is private and personal.

All this professional privacy within the work of the human service professional has other down sides in terms of the ambient absence of organizational support and supervision. Practitioners may find they are alone in trying to sort out difficult ethical issues. Donovan and Jackson (1991) refer to the lack of effective performance appraisal in human service organizations which traditionally favour 'self and peer appraisal rather than superior or subordinate oversight' (1991, p. 334) and to the problems inherent in unclear lines of accountability. Jackson and Donovan (1999, p. 93) also see this is a particular concern in small not-for-profit organizations – all the more common now with outsourcing of essential services to non-government providers – many of which 'may use peer review alone as a means of standard setting'. This moral autonomy means it is not surprising to see many authors in the counselling and interviewing field emphasizing the need for a self-aware, culturally sensitive and reflective approach to practice as discussed previously.

Gendered contexts of interviewing

Another context to consider concerns the gender of the practitioner. To some extent in much of the literature, interviewing or counselling is described as a relatively consistent or gender-neutral process, whether the interviewer is female or male. However, it is apparent that social and cultural frames and individuals' values and expectations make a difference to outcomes in some circumstances. The practitioner's gender is part of the cultural context and requires to be taken into account in examining the impact she or he has on clients in the professional relationship. The gendered aspects of nonverbal behaviour are also important but these are discussed in Chapter Two.

There are some situations where the practitioner's gender will be very significant to clients such that they may specifically ask to see a female or male worker. This request may be because some clients feel socially and culturally restrained from talking with a person of the opposite gender. As well, such a request might be issue-based in that, whereas the gender of the interviewer may not normally matter, some topics, such as those concerning sexuality, gender preference and/or health issues, might make this a matter of some sensitivity. Clients' expectations about social ideals, as discussed before, also include views about how males or females should present or behave in current society. Macho expectations of how to be male or images of perfect motherhood impinge on personal realties for many clients (Chaplin 1997, p. 270).

Recognizing the impact of gender variables on the professional interaction raises the issue of power. The practitioner role alone is imbued with considerable power in the eyes of most clients. Chaplin (1997, p. 273) suggests that paternalistic social structures that still exist may mean male interviewers 'collude very effectively', if at times unwittingly, in sustaining the myth of men as 'the experts, the all-knowing ones' – with all the power this implies. This raises images of dependent females being fixed by strong male therapists. Male counsellors and female clients may become caught up in collusive relationships in preserving power and gender myths. It is obvious there are a range of attributes attached to a person's gender, all requiring conscious management if they are not to impact negatively on outcomes of the helping interaction. Gender issues impact on a range of other factors in professional work, including promotional opportunities for women in many organizational settings.

It is important to be able to accommodate a client's request or unspoken but discernible need for a same-gender worker. If it is not possible to meet their request, then the matter needs to be discussed and the client given the option of seeking the service elsewhere if this is feasible. It is never productive to force a female client to see a male practitioner or vice versa, because someone believes it will be *good for them* (Chaplin 1997, p. 279). If there are no such options and the interview must proceed for urgent reasons, then it should be conducted with high sensitivity and full acknowledgement that the issue of the worker's gender may act as a block to progress in the interview.

Corey and Corey (1999, pp. 154–173) also point out that clients present with such a vast range of issues that these inevitably intersect with the worker's own gender-based values. Such client issues may concern abortion, relationship and parenting styles, gender roles and sexuality and a vast array of other aspects of modern lifestyles. In working with clients, interviewers often struggle to refrain from imposing own gender-based values on clients or, as discussed previously, from passing general judgement about the client's lifestyle choices.

Values and the honest and sensitive expression of these are shaped by a person's social, gender and organizational frames. Griffin (1994, pp. 422–425) and Cupach and Canary (1997, pp. 121–147) describe how an individual's cultural heritage influences all aspects of their values – sometimes without this being acknowledged. Variables of gender, ethnic background, family structure and history, age, class and complexity of life experience all influence the professional interaction and the experience of this for both workers and clients. Everyone approaches all situations from within a personal and cultural bubble, according to Corey and Corey (1999, pp. 154–173), bringing a complexity of issues related to all communication between helper and client.

Key points on professional contexts in interviewing work

➤ Contexts of practice intersect with practitioners' personal, organizational, gender and values issues

➤ Individualistic social and professional values may clash with those of clients

➤ It is important to deconstruct idealized views of the person and professional approaches

➤ The private nature of much organizational practice may limit exploration of these professional issues

➤ Gender experience influences many aspects of professional practice

➤ Culture is pervasively influential on all human interaction

CHAPTER OVERVIEW

The chapter has briefly defined the processes involved in a *single* interview when it is competently managed. As well, the features of a *three-stage* process are described as a possible progression when there is opportunity for long-term work with clients. This chapter then moved on to define a range of social, personal, values-based, managerial, gender frames surrounding professional interactions in the human services, often rendering the task before many practitioners and clients both challenging and complex. Additionally, because many clients are disillusioned and struggling to believe in the future, positive encouragement through strengths-focused perspectives is defined as important to assist clients to find paths into an improved future. All these issues raise the need for extra vigilance in the minds of professional workers as they conduct their private, invisible yet essential work. Whatever the purpose and intention of the interview, ongoing responsiveness and empathy at all points and the ability to apply these skills purposefully to achieve clients' diverse goals form the basis for competent and effective work. The ability to select skills to apply to each client's particular set of circumstances and stage of progress is the artistry of effective professional practice. Of primary importance in this is the use of a range of consistent empathic verbal responses, supported through effective nonverbal behaviours. This range of basic skills is the focus of the next chapter.

CHAPTER 2

Making the Initial Connection with Nonverbal and Verbal Skills

The key features of effective work with clients entail a range of essential skills used for interviewing in most human service settings. Primarily, these are verbal and nonverbal skills and are seen as essential throughout all stages of the interviewing process in establishing a basis for work with most clients for whatever purpose.

Essential at the beginning of an interview is the establishment of a clear understanding of the client's world from inside the client's frame of reference, which is maintained until a basis of trust is well established. The most important feature of this early work is that the focus does not move outside the client's current experiences and their feelings and perceptions about these. Such skills form the cornerstone of effective practice when established as a genuine response style of the worker. The consistent application of attentive nonverbal behaviour and reflective verbal responses encourages clients to begin to tell their stories – who they are in their current life – and provides an empathic structure that facilitates the progression of clients' understanding of self over time. By the end of this chapter it is expected that the reader will have a basic understanding of a basic range of nonverbal and verbal skills used in effectively managing an interview and be able to differentiate reflective responses from those that are not.

First, this chapter focuses on nonverbal behaviours to assist in establishing and maintaining focus and in demonstrating the interviewer's attention on the client.

Nonverbal skills: key processes in connecting

Surrounding a person's ability to respond empathically is a set of skills and processes usually referred to as *attending*, *observing* and *listening*. *Attending* is physical, psychological and cognitive as is *observing*. *Listening* is a psychological, cognitive or mind function, entailing a focus on the client's verbal expression. The functions of attending and observing thus support the listening process by assisting the practitioner to notice all aspects of the client's behaviour. This comes to the attending, observing and listening interviewer as a flow of data from the client, providing a wealth of information from which a response can be formed – one that demonstrates empathy and sensitivity to the client's ideas and feelings. The demonstration of the efficacy of attending, observing and listening skills is through their impact on effective reflective verbal responses. These demonstrate that the key issues and feelings, spoken about and expressed nonverbally by the client, have been picked up. So these cognitive, psychological and nonverbal processes of attending and observing and listening provide the basis for the interviewer's verbal competence. Before looking more closely at these nonverbal behaviours, it is important to acknowledge here that nonverbal behaviours are not culturally neutral and that their social and cultural significance and their impact is often overlooked.

The unspoken realm of communication

Theorists such as Stack, Hill and Hickson (1991, p. 43) suggest that up to 70 per cent of the emotional meaning of our communication is conveyed through nonverbal channels although they suggest that nonverbal communication is a largely neglected aspect of what occurs when people communicate. They cite Ekman and Friesen (1969) in noting that 'Most people do not know what they are doing with their bodies when they are talking, and no one tells them' (Stacks et al. 1991, p. 44). Gudykunst and Kim (1997, p. 234) affirm this view and cite Hall (1966) in noting that nonverbal communication is largely unconscious for most individuals. Nonetheless, as people communicate, they both absorb and emit a huge mass of information through nonverbal channels.

Although nonverbal behaviour is such a meaningful source of information, particularly about how a person feels, it is often ignored, down-played or misinterpreted during the communication process. At times, people pick up emotional messages from nonverbal signals but are constrained from dealing with this information in an open and honest manner. This is partly due to a lack of conscious awareness of the messages and because it may be socially unacceptable to make overt that which is conveyed nonverbally – especially if this is involuntary in nature, which is often the case. Effective counsellors have a higher level of awareness about nonverbal information flowing to and from their clients. The ability to read clients' nonverbal behaviour is a very important tool in professional interviewing. However, it is important to remember that clients also read *interviewers'* nonverbal communication, which is why it is vital to be cognizant of managing one's nonverbal self in this area.

Gender and culture in nonverbal communication

How the practitioner behaves nonverbally is largely a product of their background and of their culture and gender. Pearson, West and Turner (1995, pp. 119–127) focus on gender differences in respect to *proxemics* in nonverbal communication. Proxemics refers to how men and women use *space*, how close they choose to sit with another person and how comfortable they feel with being close. Pearson et al. (1995, p. 119) suggest that both males and females are likely to be upset or offended when others stand or sit too far away, more than when they are too close. However, women tolerate less closeness than do men, although high self-concept people of both genders are more comfortable being close. They also refer to *kinesics*, which is how men and women use *body movement*, for instance, body posture and bearing, gesture, facial expression and eye contact. Women tend to use less space then do men, often sitting with legs closed and arms close to the body, whereas men are more inclined to extend their legs – both lengthwise and apart (Pearson et al. 1995, p. 126). This may mean male body positioning offends some female clients. Females tend to fiddle with their hair or clothing although generally they use fewer gestures than males, who are more likely to use expansive hand and arm moments, crack their knuckles and engage in more leg movements and foot tapping (Pearson et al. 1995, p. 127). In general, the material from Pearson et al. (1995, pp. 125–127) can be taken to suggest that female interviewers more often need to consider sitting in an open posture and to avoid fiddling, whereas males need more vigilance about invading clients' space with leg positioning and movement and hand gestures.

As well as gender, other aspects of culture may be significant in managing nonverbal behaviour within the interview situation. Kinesic and proxemic aspects of communication are important in dealing with clients from different ethnic groups. Gudykunst and Kim (1997, p. 226) suggest nonverbal behaviours can be very culturally specific and so may have impact on the outcomes of an interviewing session without the worker being aware of this. Cultural norms about space or eye contact between genders may impact on the comfort of the client in discussing their issues. So, all of the ideas about nonverbal attending in interviewing need to be considered within a context that includes cultural differences, as well as those related to gender. Competent nonverbal behaviour is about interviewers orienting themselves physically, psychologically and culturally in relating to another person. The range of cultural and ethnic expectations about courteous and acceptable nonverbal behaviour between clients and practitioners and between males and females is too vast to fully describe here. Suffice it to say, that both male and female counsellors require a heightened awareness of their own nonverbal presentation. In general then, the following guidelines can be followed in most interviews, but at times aspects may need to be adjusted for work with some clients from particular cultural backgrounds.

Effective nonverbal behaviour in the interview

Managing nonverbal behaviour is vital as it provides a two-way flow of information between worker and client. It is essential to observe how the client sits and behaves as a source of information about their feelings and general receptiveness in the interview process. All counsellors need to manage their own nonverbal behaviour to present a receptive presence to clients. Egan (2007, pp. 75–78) uses the acronym SOLER to refer to nonverbal qualities of the interviewer in terms of the *attending* position. The S refers to *squaring off*, the O to using an *open posture*, the L to *leaning* toward the client, the E for *eye contact* and the R for a *relaxed* or natural use of the preceding behaviours.

Expanding on the five features in SOLER, Egan (2007, p. 74) refers to eight aspects of nonverbal behaviour that together facilitate the flow of information between two people talking with each other. Egan describes these as the following:

- Body behaviour is about all aspects of body posture and movement, including hand gestures, arm and leg positions and movements, head nods and all other shift and moves

- Eye behaviour is about eye contact, eye gaze and intensity, eye direction and eye movements
- Facial expressions include smiles, frowns and raised eyebrows
- Voice features means tonality of voice, volume, clarity, inflection, use of silences, spaces between words, sighs and other vocalizations
- Observable autonomic physiological responses include quickened or more audible breathing, blushing, paleness, pupil dilation or observable facial or body perspiration
- Physical characteristics are about aspects of fitness, height, weight, complexion, and attractiveness
- Space refers to how close or far interviewer and client are from each other
- General appearance and presentation include grooming and dress. This also includes perfume use and other body odours and/or breath smells from halitosis, garlic, cigarettes or alcohol.

Ivey and Ivey (2003, p. 43) refer to the nonverbal realm as comprising 'The Three V's + B'. The three 'V's of attending include 'visual/eye contact' (p. 43), 'vocal qualities' (pp. 44–45) and 'verbal tracking' (p. 45). The 'B' refers to body language – in particular body orientation and body use, particularly 'authentic body language' (pp. 46–48). The vocal qualities referred to by Ivey and Ivey (2003) encompass vocal tone, speech rate and verbal tracking – all related to staying with and remaining focused on the client in an attentive and flexible manner. The qualities referred to overall by Ivey and Ivey (2003) pick up on most of Egan's points except for those referring to physical characteristics and appearance, a set of characteristics about which to be mindful, as most helping practitioners work in close proximity to their clients.

Consider how people sit when they are really interested in a television program, such as a sports grand final or a really interesting drama. People often demonstrate excellent physical and psychological attending behaviour in such settings. The person leans forward, perhaps even on the edge of the chair. The sitting position is usually open, rather than folded in, eye contact is strongly focused on the action on the screen and facial expressions might mirror what happens as the game or drama unfolds. In other words, the person demonstrates absolute concentration and this is the epitome of good psychological attending behaviour. Now, in the TV-watching incident described here, there may also be much arm waving and shouting of encouragement for the favoured side and insults may be hurled which would not be appropriate in an interviewing situation! But if this scenario is calmed down a little, what we have is a version of excellent attending.

The classic nonverbal attending position

In the classic position, the person sits in a relaxed forward-leaning position – with their upper body forming a kind of triangle between back, legs and arms. The S and O of Egan's acronym of SOLER refer to how, where possible, the practitioner sits *square on* to the client, oriented *openly* towards the client with both feet on the floor, legs not crossed and arms unfolded. The optimum is where client and worker can sit face to face. The interviewer's hands should rest comfortably on knees, upper legs or in the lap. Some people like to keep their hands together loosely to limit unconscious hand gestures, but it is important not to let this develop into anxious white-knuckled hand clasping. Now obviously, at times this square on position is not feasible, such as when an interaction occurs whilst standing next to a person, whilst walking together outside or sitting together on a bench or on a sofa. When such circumstances occur, the practitioner will need to adapt the classic SOLER attending characteristics but still attempt to retain as many features as possible.

Furniture and physical surrounding for interviewing

To facilitate an open and forward-leaning posture, it may be necessary to locate furniture that suits the worker's body type as well as the client's. For instance, some chairs may not allow short interviewers to sit comfortably with their feet firmly on the floor. The chair that the interviewer sits on also needs to be more or less the *same* height as the client's, to result in both practitioner and client sitting at the same level. The intention is to avoid any height differences that may leave the worker sitting *over* or *under* the gaze of the client. Short females may find that higher-heeled footwear helps feet to remain on the floor. Sometimes the use of a low footstool may compensate for both poor furniture design and short legs. If the furniture forces some variation in the classic attending position, it will be all the more important to pay attention to other aspects such as eye contact, keeping arms in a relaxed open position and maintaining an overall, square-on, open orientation.

Sometimes it will also not be possible to sit on two chairs more or less facing each other. The counsellor may wish to sit on the floor or ground for instance when talking with a small child. The only furniture available in some settings, such as the client's house, might be a sofa where it seems appropriate to sit alongside each other. If these things happen, it is vital to keep the remaining features of attending in place such as body orientation and face-to-face eye contact/gaze (by turning as much as possible towards the client) to demonstrate attention and to facilitate good observation of the client's facial expression and body posture. It may also be important to manage distracting environmental factors – such as noise from nearby people, radios, and so on; clients' or other people's crying children, barking dogs and so on; the stuffiness of the room; and uncomfortable chairs. The addition of a whiteboard or large pieces of paper attached to an easel facilitates the making of visible notes on these, to emphasize key points during the interview. In taking charge of the physical surroundings, the aim is to facilitate the interviewer's attentive presence, the comfort of both client and worker and the management of any interferences with the interviewer's ability to maintain the classic SOLER position as described by Egan (2007).

Avoiding physical barriers

As part of maintaining an *open posture* and in selecting appropriate use of furniture, it is suggested that there are no physical objects such as a table or any other barrier between worker and client. This means not sitting at a desk with the client on the other side of it, as this conjures up images of old-fashioned medical models and ideas about expert power over clients. There are power issues implicit anyway in the views clients have about consulting a professional for assistance. Managing conditions in the room, including disposition of the furniture, in beginning the interview sends a message about considering the needs of clients and establishing the idea of a *working alliance* (Egan 2007, pp. 49–51).

Forward body lean

The L of Egan's acronym refers to the forward lean of the worker's body towards the client. In general, the angle of the interviewer's back should be such that the upper body is leaning forward slightly – in the client's direction. Clients may vary in their own seating position and we cannot expect perfect SOLER behaviour from them. The furniture has importance in this issue of body lean too. Some chairs, such as lounge chairs have a reverse back support making it hard to sit forward comfortably. Where feasible, these may need to be exchanged for more upright if less cosy chairs. If this is not possible, the worker may need to perch forward on the chair but in doing so to avoid the 'about to pounce' look. In general, the angle of the practitioner's lean towards the client should be maintained, along with an open and face to face posture, unblocked by furniture. It is also necessary to consider other features such as the amount of space available between the two chairs.

Space considerations in body positioning

It is important not to encroach on the personal space of clients and for both clients and interviewers to feel comfortable about the distance between them. People from different cultural groups have a range of space preferences, so distance between chairs may need adapting case by case. Burgoon, Buller and Woodall (1996, pp. 91–92) suggest that the span of distance between people who are engaged in social communication is between 4 to 10 feet (or from 1 to 2 metres). As the interview situation is a more personal social contact, this usually means the space is at the bottom end of this range – that is, around a metre. Note that this is the distance between heads if both people were sitting in the classic attending position. Nelson-Jones (1997, p. 104) sees the head-to-head distance as being between 1 and 1.5 metres in most Western cultures. Ivey and Ivey (2003, pp. 105) describe the distance, accepted in 'European American tradition,' as 'arms length'. Most thus seem to agree on the distance. Generally, the space between practitioner and client should allow quiet levels of speech volume. This means that clients, anxious about confidentiality, are less likely to fear being overheard and that occasional hand-to-hand touch is possible, if this is situationally, socially and culturally appropriate. Of course, this distance varies according to different cultural perspectives and establishing ground rules on this issue of space requires some good observation, knowledge about space norms in other cultural groups, the flexibility to adjust furniture if needed and the ability to negotiate when it is unclear what is most appropriate.

As an added thought here, it is probably apparent now that the optimum attending position entails being in relatively close proximity with clients. This calls for good personal hygiene on the interviewer's part. If clients have not been quite so attentive to their personal freshness, practitioners may need to exercise professional self-restraint and personal equanimity.

Use of eye contact and qualities of eye gaze

The E of Egan's acronym refers to eye contact. Nelson-Jones (1997, p. 103) discusses eye contact in reference to *gaze*, or the broader set of processes about how we look at people and this is important. He warns against staring, which may unwittingly convey messages about dominance or power positioning. People from some cultural groups may have different nonverbal norms about eye contact. For example, cultural rules may exist in some ethnic groups about males and females engaging in mutual eye gazing. Additionally, culture aside, many clients may not wish to, or may find it difficult to return eye contact. Poor self-esteem, anxiety and fear may lessen a person's comfort with eye-to-eye gazing. So it is the worker's *own* eye behaviour that needs managing – not the client's.

In general eye contact is gentle rather than intense. The position of the head is vital as this determines the *direction* of the eye gaze. If the head is thrown back, even slightly, the practitioner is likely to be looking down her nose at the client, perhaps unintentionally conveying some arrogance or superiority to the client. Likewise if the chin is dropped towards the chest even slightly and this tilts the head down, then the upward gaze widens the eye and may come across to the client as submissive, coy or even seductive. A sideways angle of eye gaze may convey disbelief or scepticism. To avoid these accidental messages being conveyed to the client, it is important to aim for level eye gaze in most interview settings.

Relaxed use of attending functions

The final letter in Egan's acronym is R for relaxed, referring to a 'relatively relaxed or natural' use of all the previous aspects (Egan 2007, p. 76), that is, in sitting about a metre apart with a square, open position, leaning forward and maintaining consistent and level eye gaze. Learning to sit in this attending position in a natural way can be a challenge, especially when practitioners feel anxious about doing the right thing and when they are learning and/or being observed. There needs to be a balance between ignoring own nonverbal behaviours and being so preoccupied with physical self to the extent of becoming frozen with anxiety and unable to focus on or hear what the client says. Much practice and feedback usually provides the remedy. This relaxation – or lack of it – relates as well to facial expression, hand gestures and other body movements and the use, or overuse, of head nodding.

Facial expression

A reasonably natural, benign facial expression is the norm for the professional listener as the interview starts. Facial expression may shift later depending on what is being discussed. The discussion of very dramatic or sad events may lead the worker to look sad or more serious. Alternatively, references to good news, the recalling of happy events or the occurrence of funny moments during an interview call for a lightening of expression, smiling and on occasions outright laughter.

Smiling can be a professional bad habit however and some people may find from feedback and heightened self-awareness that they need to work at reserving smiling for more intentional purposes in the interview. A smile is usually appropriate in meeting the client but after that care needs to be taken to reserve it for special moments. Overuse of smiling may be a female habit – referred to as social smiling—although males also engage in this. Pearson et al. (1995, p. 123) say that women smile more than men and that many women, particularly those from the middle classes of Western societies, see the smile as an interaction device, used to keep the conversation going – and to some extent it may work this way. But some people smile fairly incessantly, through sad and bad moments as well as happy ones and the smile loses its power when this happens. Ivey and Ivey (2003, p. 105) accept that 'smiling is a sign of warmth in most cultures' but point out that in some it may not be. They mention the traditional Japanese culture in particular where smiling may be interpreted as a sign of social discomfort, which it can be in many human service interview settings too! So after the meeting and greeting stage is over, reserve smiling for when it is appropriate to the content of the client's narrative or for light-hearted moments in the interaction.

Hand gestures and other body movements

The anxiety inherent in the interview setting, both in practice and in the reality of professional work, may engender a range of facial expressions including nervous smiling. As well, body movements in the form of gestures, habitual actions such as scratching, hair twiddling, hand rubbing and foot jiggling may all be unintentional displays of the worker's feelings. Likewise, shifting body positions may signal discomfort, distraction and irritation or a number of other reactions to the client or the situation. Some exception to this exists when a process termed mirroring occurs (Geldard 1999, p. 62, 63) which is where counsellors shift their body on occasions to deliberately match that of the client. This matching, for example sitting on the edge of the chair to mirror the anxious client and then moving back to a less tense position may encourage clients to become more aware of own tension and also sit back and relax a little. Learning to deliberately and intentionally manage body movements and gestures is a necessary part of becoming a competent interviewer.

Head nodding

In an attempt to show attention and interest, inexperienced counsellors, especially those who feel keen to appear friendly and encouraging, often overuse head nodding. This is easily observed in a video of the interaction and consequently practice with the use of a video recording is highly recommended to iron out the wrinkles in a person's nonverbal presence, especially the overuse of head nodding. A few head nods can provide a powerful reinforcement for clients. For instance, when a client focuses more clearly after rambling, a nod or two can reinforce this positive change. Nodding needs to be used sparingly however, if it is to retain its impact for this purpose. Interviewers, who nod incessantly in response to everything said, have fewer options when they wish to encourage the client nonverbally to stay with an issue.

In general then, the practitioner's own focused presence is supported by being personally aware and managing own nonverbal presence and by contributing a peaceful interview setting with a minimum of distracting aspects – for both counsellor and client. It is clear then that in maintaining a warm and focused presence the physical presentation of interviewers needs to be kept under a fairly high degree of self-management, as does their internal state.

Psychological attending

In addition to the importance of effective physical positioning, good listening and attending is also dependent on adopting a focused psychological approach involving keen observation of the client. The two processes of attending and observing are both physical and psychological – and feed into each other. When a person sits attentively and keeps her eye gaze appropriately focused on the client, it is more likely that she will focus psychologically and be able to observe the client. Of course, this is not guaranteed. Managing own anxiety, quietening internal dialogue and focusing energies can be quite challenging. The processes of psychological attending and observing involve the following:

- Limiting internal dialogue about what to say next and about other things on the interviewer's mind
- Steady breathing and relaxing into an attentive but comfortable position
- Focusing on psychological listening and observing
- Giving full attention to the client and working at being interested in this person
- Listening to and considering the meaning of the client's narrative
- Considering what is being conveyed through voice tone, pace, breathing of the client
- Observing the client's facial expressions, gestures, body positioning
- Observing any other nonverbal behaviour or body changes of the client

All of these processes help the worker to maintain an internal attentive silence while the client is speaking. It may be necessary to resist working out what to say next until the client seems to have completed a thought or idea. This is a real challenge and most students I have worked with struggle with the pressure to mentally compose a response before they have heard it all. When workers feel anxious about getting the response right and expressed at the right time, performance pressure may block their ability to maintain a calm, open mind towards the client.

Bankart (1997, p. 301) considers the best kind of psychological attending is akin to a Zen–like concentration, where the client becomes the only focus for the worker. This means being able to control self-consciousness about physical attending and to quieten internal dialogues about what to say next. This entails bringing all conscious thought processes under self-control and learning to maintain active, focused attention on the client – without becoming self-preoccupied. Those who practice meditation may find it useful to apply these principles to the mind quieting process in interviewing. For many it requires practice.

Unfortunately, internal functions of concentration and psychological focusing are hard for another person to give feedback on. There may be something in the nature of the eye gaze for example that will indicate the practitioner is letting thoughts stray. Of course, the proof of undivided attention, observation and listening will be demonstrated in the quality of the response as in its accuracy and responsiveness to the client's issues.

Sometimes non–focusing is attributable to anxiety, or to finding it hard to like clients or to understand them. Whatever the reason, when attention wanders the counsellor may miss what the client says, or mis-read the connection between issues and themes. Learning to relax into attending, observing and listening is an important part of improving the ability to focus. Another feature of non–focusing shows in deliberate attempts to distract the client from their own issues because the practitioner – either consciously or unconsciously – finds these uncomfortable to discuss. Here the client's words may be heard but attempts are made to change the topic, focus on more pleasant things, or talk about workers' own issues. These and other blocks to effective responding are discussed later in this chapter.

Following skills in the counselling interview

Following skills may be relatively habitual sub-verbal behaviours when people are in conversation with each other. In interviewing, these little pieces of behaviour encourage the client to go on speaking. They reinforce other nonverbal messages that the interviewer is staying with the client and remains attentive to their issues as they tell their story. They usually comprise the following:

Verbal 'door openers'

This category includes invitations to begin – for example an initial open question like 'Where shall we start?' Nonverbal behaviours – these consisting of eye contact, body lean and so on – also encourage the client to begin to speak.

Occasional sub-verbal sounds

These small sounds, like 'Uh-hu' or 'Mmm' may encourage the client to continue and can be usefully applied especially when the interviewer wishes to hear more before responding. None of these *sounds* replaces good reflective responding in encouraging the client to explore issues or to recount their stories thoughtfully. Managing the frequency of these sounds is part of monitoring own behaviours and bringing unconscious processes under more conscious control. Constant nodding or repeating a word or sound is often distracting to clients. The recording of an interview interaction on video tape will demonstrate frequency of habitual use of sounds.

In addition, exclamations like 'Great!', 'Wonderful!', 'Wow!', 'Terrific!' and 'Gosh!' or 'Cool' need managing as these all display some sort of approval or exaggerated interest that will not be taken as genuine by many clients. As well, these effusive exclamations may dissuade some clients from talking about the less *wonderful* or not at all *cool* parts of their world. Likewise, verbal habits like beginning each response with 'So ...' can also be distracting to clients.

Minimal reflections

At times, a short restatement of a very small piece of the client's spoken material happens and this is termed a *minimal reflection*. It is minimal because all it catches is a small piece of what the client says but it is done in the spirit of reflection. It occurs sometimes because the client goes on at length but at other times it is all the interviewer can manage due to own confusion or inattention.

As an example, a client says, 'There is just not enough to go around. I always seem to run out of money before the end of the fortnight. And then I have to borrow from my friends. It seems impossible – I can't seem to get on top of it and I am not a bad manager of money really – well I am sometimes but basically I cope'. The interviewer says 'borrowing from friends', or 'cope somehow'. It shows the interviewer heard something and is trying to stay in touch, but does not reflect much of what was said. There is the problem that a minimal reflection may not even catch a central piece of the narrative. So when just a couple of words or a single word is all that is possible, this very minimalist response may work only as a form of 'follower' – that is to encourage the client to keep talking. In other words it cannot be seen as empathic or demonstrating much understanding of the client's narrative.

Generally these minimal reflections are best avoided. It is better to wait until there is a space to formulate a paraphrase, or if there is no opportunity to do so because the client is very talkative, to courteously interrupt to explain the importance of the interviewer's responses to the success of the interview. It also needs to be noted here that a minimal reflection may have the same impact as a question or other probe if an inquiring or tentative intonation is used – like *'Not enough then?'* Even accidental questions, brought about by this intonation, act as probes in prodding the client instead of showing empathy and staying with their narrative.

Appropriate attentive silence

Finally one of the best 'following' skills is attentive silence. It is essential that interviewers learn to sit in silence with a client and to resist the need to fill even small conversational spaces, especially by asking questions. This is challenging as many individuals have a low tolerance for conversational silence. An active sort of silence means that while sitting in silence the interviewer observes the client closely, maintains gentle eye contact, keeps body position and movement under control and maintains a slight forward lean with open posture. Most individuals think a period of silence is longer than it is in reality and have poor tolerance for it.

All of the preceding is beginning to underline how *intentional* the interviewing process needs to be and how many things need managing to keep up a focused listening stance. The range of nonverbal processes has been described as functions that interviewers need to place under their personal control. I stress here, however, that all these aspects of personal presentation and behaviour are able to be learned, which I feel is a more comforting belief than any idea that competent interviewers are born rather than made. Competent interviewers are products of reading, reflection, skills practice, reflection, feedback, more practice, reflection and reading – and continual reflexive learning. Now the focus moves onto verbal responses – the things we say!

Key points on nonverbal behaviour in interviewing

➤ Maintain appropriate space between client and interviewer

➤ Sit in a relatively open position – no folded arms or legs

➤ Manage gendered habits of nonverbal style

➤ Sit leaning toward the client

➤ Maintain a level eye gaze and offer consistent eye contact

➤ Keep hand gestures and other body movement to a minimum

➤ Use nodding occasionally to reinforce aspects of client narrative

➤ Attend psychologically and focus the mind on the task

➤ Monitor the use of 'followers' such as sub-vocals

➤ Develop tolerance for sitting in silence

➤ Combine all these functions in an integrated and natural style

Verbal foundations of empathic responding

Of course, the skill repertoire of competent interviewers also includes verbal responses and these, in their best form, demonstrate consistent empathic appreciation of what the client has expressed. The material forming the foundation of empathic verbal responses comes from focused attending, observing and from listening to the client's expression of ideas and feelings. A consistent pattern of reflections and other empathic responses, when established in the behavioural repertoire of the practitioner and applied deliberately, provides a stable set of skills for managing most events throughout an interview.

Maintaining the reflective approach

In establishing a professional relationship, getting the interview underway, and encouraging the client to narrate their story, an empathic reflective approach is the mainstay of the competent interviewer. Whenever an interviewer feels overwhelmed or confused at the start of an interview, a period of silence, with appropriate eye gaze and physical positioning, buys time and focuses the mind. Then, after personal composure has been regained, a response may be appropriate, reflecting something the client has expressed in words or nonverbally. This focusing approach helps interviewers resist temptations to give advice, make irrelevant comments, suggest solutions or ask unnecessary questions.

By the end of this chapter, it is hoped readers will appreciate the difference between reflective responses and other types of responses that do not demonstrate empathy – termed 'roadblocks'. The reason reflective responses are so emphasized is that most people will talk quite freely if they are offered non-judgemental, accepting and warm responses from a person who demonstrates attentive nonverbal behaviour and genuine interest in the client's issues. A central point here is that good listeners put the focus on the other person and on what they are offering, rather than asking for additional information, or talking about other things. Look at the following client statement:

> Well I don't have a lot left over after I pay the rent. The benefit doesn't leave a lot of spare money after the necessities are bought. I try to put a bit aside, but it has been a struggle. I worry about how to make do and wake up in the night sometimes thinking 'I can't keep making it work'. I know this is not helping me or the situation much – to worry about it like this, and I do cope somehow – just barely some months – but so far I'm holding it together.

At times, a simple reflection catches a piece of what the client says. An example might be *'Money's really tight'*, or *'You're holding it together'* (that includes a positive frame also), or *'There's not a lot left after the rent's paid'*. A reflection is usually just an aspect or slice of what has been said by the client. It shows some understanding, but does not encompass the whole situation. There is clearly a lot of choice about what to pick up on and usually it is best to take an aspect that seems fairly central and the client will probably want to say more about. Where possible, a positive behaviour will encourage and affirm the client as opposed to focusing on the problems or the difficult things. *'You are holding it together'* for instance is a positive behaviour reflection, rather than '*You are having problems in making it work*'. Sometimes just a couple of words or a single word is enough to show some understanding and this very minimalist reflection can also work like a sort of 'follower' to encourage the client to keep talking. So, examples here would be something like *'You cope'*. Just a note here: be mindful not to make short reflections into closed questions by putting a questioning intonation at the end, and do be aware of their selectivity.

The value of empathic responding flows to both the person being listened to and the listener, as the use of empathy reinforces the professional relationship. When the interviewer demonstrates genuine interest in the client's world, they feel more interesting and valued and self-esteem improves. Over time within this accepting environment, clients develop trust and greater confidence and begin to sort out issues for themselves by locating their own solutions to their current concerns.

One of the major challenges in attempting to formulate reflective responses is the struggle many interviewers experience in not introducing anything new and remaining focused on the meaning of clients' expression, both verbally and nonverbally. Empathic reflections pick up central pieces of meaning out of the client's expression, focusing on the present moment in terms of the client's story. Empathy never comes in the form of a question (as questions ask for new information or redirect the client) nor advice (which attempt to solve things on behalf of the client or to tell her or him how they should feel, think and behave).

Empathic reflective responses come in all shapes and forms of *statements* – although not usually questions – and are characterized by their focus on aspects of the client's verbal and nonverbal messages. Reflective responses capture, in the worker's words, a feature of the meaning expressed in the client's narrative. Effective responses focus empathically on clients' *feelings*, on parts of their *situations* as described and sometimes on what the client is doing in these situations – their *behaviour*. Accurate reflective responses demonstrate that the worker has heard and understood the important aspects of the client's story about their world. In the following example, the practitioner offers only a question on an issue not really mentioned instead of responding to what has been said.

> **Client:** I've been working there for seven years now and I feel a bit stuck. But the idea of moving on scares me. I know that a job is just what one makes it, and probably I am doing as well as I'm likely to anywhere else. I mean it's a good job, it pays well and I have some good friends there, so why would I want to chuck all that in? But there are some little niggles – like time's running out and perhaps I need to push myself a bit before it's too late.
>
> **Practitioner:** How much do you earn a week?

What a deficient response! Can you see this? It is too directive and intrusive and does not show that much has been heard. As well none of the feelings are picked up, such as the client's overall ambivalence. If this pattern persists over several responses, the client will feel less and less like exploring feelings and ideas. Instead even a brief response such as: '*The job is secure but unchallenging*' would provide some assurance that the client has been heard and understood.

The concept of active empathy

Effective, empathic interviewers are deliberate, purposeful and *active*. Effective listening is not just a matter of nodding and murmuring 'right' or 'mmm' as long as the client is talking. Competent interviewers are not passive at all and even when silent, they listen actively. They verbally respond – frequently – with brief, empathic reflections and paraphrases. Ivey and Ivey (2003, p. 125) and Egan (2007, pp. 116, 117) stress the importance of the interviewer using frequent but brief paraphrases to assist the client's focus and to demonstrate actively their own focused attention to the client's issues and feelings. When interviewers are active and alert it demonstrates they are keen to understand the client's ideas and beliefs.

Occasionally this might mean stopping the client, by saying something like 'I'll ask you pause there so I can check I understand you. I'm picking up that you feel fairly overwhelmed because the kids have been sick and it's been stressful coping with your new job'. Empathic work is active and focused on the client's current feelings and perceptions. In other words, the responsive and active practitioner does not allow the client to drown them both in an endless stream of words or to deflect the purposeful practitioner from responding. Instead, she sensitively intervenes to produce a meaningful dialogue – responding briefly and empathically to help to focus the client.

Key points about reflective responding

➤ Reflective work is about empathically appreciating the client's ideas without imposing own frames of reference on these

➤ When clients are responded to reflectively and positively, they feel affirmed

➤ Stay focused in the immediate situation and do not introduce new material

➤ Attempt an empathic response, even if it is brief or incomplete,

➤ Brief reflective responses are preferable to unnecessary questioning

➤ Effective interviewers are active, not passive

➤ Brief and frequent reflective responses help both verbose and silent clients to focus

---

Reaching for shared meaning in the interpreted interview

The needs of many non-English-speaking clients, as well as those with hearing difficulties or other communication problems, are often not met within the interview unless the support of an interpreter is gained.

Timmins (2002) for instance reviewed the USA-based biomedical journals from 1990 to 2000 for mention of language barriers in health care with Hispanic patients. Alarmingly, it was found that significant detrimental effects of language barriers impacted on quality of care, including misdiagnosis, prescription of inappropriate medications, lack of patient information leading to poor compliance, lack of follow-up and a decrease in preventive services. Without interpreter support, the client with a language or hearing need may not be able to be understood well and quality and appropriateness of service provision will be jeopardized.

Ensuring equivalent understanding of meaning is in some doubt at the best of times, even when practitioner and client share a language. This doubt is magnified however, in working with interpreters in interviewing clients, especially given the interpreter's natural tendency to *paraphrase* what is essentially already paraphrased material from the interviewer. This means there may be quite a gulf between the interviewer's and clients' intended meaning deriving from the interpreter's translation of equivalent meaning. Kvale (1989, p. 85) notes the 'basic issue of communicative validity' is a feature in both the interviewer's and the interpreter's efforts to correctly understand the meaning of clients – and the importance of each understanding the other. If this is in doubt, then the whole issue of empathy is under threat as is the veracity of the information gained through the interaction.

To maximize the accuracy of the translation process, it is advisable that practitioners avoid the temptation to use bilingual agency staff or client's family members or friends as interpreters. This is partly because confidentiality may be compromised but as Flores et al. (2003) suggest for added reasons of interpreter competence. It is important to be aware that errors of interpretation are possible in using the services of well-trained interpreters but that these occur more frequently, often at quite serious levels of inaccuracy, with *ad hoc* interpreters such as family members, friends or other bi-lingual workers who lack interpreter training (Flores et al. 2003). So in general, the use of non-professionally trained interpreters and especially bi-lingual friends and family is best avoided, despite many clients wishing to use these people.

Background issues to consider in using an interpreter

To ensure goodness of fit between the interpreter and the practitioner's and the client's needs, the skills, qualifications and background of the interpreter should be thoroughly researched. The client's culture should be considered also, not only in reference to using appropriate interpreters but also on issues like acceptable dress code and use of eye contact both between and within genders for example. Pareek and Rao (1980, p. 166) emphasize the importance of cultural familiarity in order to conduct interviews in a foreign language, suggesting that cultural norms should be respected to support channels of communication. Willcox (2006) suggests that 'counselling work with the Deaf could be classed as trans-cultural or cross-cultural counselling. Any hearing counsellor working with a Deaf client needs to have knowledge and understanding of Deaf culture'. The interviewer should also not make assumptions about the client's language on the basis of their nationality either. For instance, some Vietnamese people speak a Chinese dialect rather than Vietnamese.

In considering a suitable interpreter, Pareek and Rao (1980, p. 165) note that 'Unless the interpreter is well acquainted with the various topics of the interview, he is not likely to be effective'. This suggests a meeting between the interviewer and the interpreter before the encounter with the client or at least some phone or email contact to discuss key issues. Kvale (1996, p. 148) seems to agree with this, stating that the interpreter needs 'an extensive knowledge of the interview theme' so he or she is capable of conducting an 'informed conversation about the topic' and that to be able to manage this 'will know what issues are important to pursue, without attempting to shine with his or her extensive knowledge'. It is worth considering that an interpreter has considerable power within the triangular relationship, as without them no interview can proceed as they hold the meaning of the conversation in their hands.

Some background research on the interpreter's knowledge and style is obviously required. Research on the client's attitudes about some other issues is also important. A consumer may express doubt about using an interpreter because of fears about costs. Normally the host organization pays the costs of employing an interpreter but check this is so before arranging the interview so the client is informed in advance about any expenses involved. As well, reassure clients about the gender and nationality of the interpreter if this is of concern to them. Anxiety about confidentiality or fear of interrogation means the interviewer needs to find ways to reassure on these matters too. Clients have the right to request a specific (qualified) interpreter and to know their full name. It is sometimes very difficult for a client to terminate an interpreted interview.

Clients might feel most constrained from telling the interpreter who is their only means of verbal communication. It can be important then to agree on a nonverbal sign to allow the client to stop the interview at any time should they feel uncomfortable as this enables them some control over proceedings. Sometimes the practitioner may feel like they lose control over the process as well however. Gaveaux (2006 online) who has worked with asylum seekers for some years, admits that sometimes

> The interpreter seems to be leading the session, which looks like a cross-examination. I think of Buber and I am filled with despair: how can I ever experience the healing of an I – Thou moment in this overcrowded setting? I have to process not only the countertransference with the client but also with the interpreter. I also have to bear in mind that some interpreters have themselves gone through devastating and damaging experiences that can come into play in the triangle.

Language needs to be clear throughout and pace of speech needs to be maintained at a moderately slow rate. As the interview gets underway, it is important to allow the interpreter ample time to finish translating for the client after each statement before the interviewer commences a new response – in other words not to interrupt the interpreter. Jargon and complicated language obviously need to be avoided in all interviews but especially so to ensure accurate translation of the interpreted interaction. Overall, the interpreted interview is imbued with a heady mixture of trust and doubt that puts under sharp examination the efficacy of the interviewing process. A consistent use of empathic reflections and attentive body language is the only consistent if faulty resource.

Key points about the interpreted interview

➤ Interpreters can help clients with a language or hearing need to be better understood

➤ Interviewing with the help of an interpreter has some impact on accurate transfer of meaning

➤ Using bilingual but untrained agency staff or family and friends of the client as interpreters is to be avoided for reasons of confidentiality and levels of competence

➤ The qualifications of the interpreter and the client's and interpreter's culture should be researched

➤ Eye contact and direction of conversation is from interviewer to client, not interpreter

➤ The power of the interpreter is a fact and needs consideration

➤ Pace is important to ensure time is allowed for the translation processes

➤ A combination of empathic reflection and attentive body language is the only practitioner resource

Roadblocks to empathic interview management

The antithesis of an empathic reflection is where the worker talks about him/herself instead of responding to the client's world. Referred to by Gordon (1970) in Miller and Rollnick (2002, p. 68) as 'roadblocks', these divert, block or actually prevent or deter the client from exploring their own important issues. The most common ones are demonstrated in the following discussion.

Many things that are expressed without much thought in normal conversation often also find their way into the helping interview. Miller and Rollnick (2002, p. 68) refer to a range of ineffective response patterns, all of which are seen as major obstructions to reflective work with clients. Roadblocks are verbal patterns that imply to some extent that the interviewer has all the answers. It is useful to consider the ways in which these are all non-reflective and how they impact on clients, getting in the way of their free exploration. There are twelve identified roadblocks, as explained in the following.

Ordering, directing or commanding

These sorts of statements often command clients *not* to feel or think something as in: '*Don't feel like that – there's no sense in getting angry*' or to do something as in: '*Try controlling yourself*'. This category of non-reflective statement comprises one of the least empathic and most impolite reactions of interviewers. They rely for their impact on the *power* of the professional, from actual roles, such as in being a teacher, boss or other authority figure or in the inherent authority a client attributes to a more educated and knowledgeable person such as a social worker or psychologist.

Warning, cautioning or threatening

This sort of non-reflection is a kind of malevolent prediction, where the interviewer makes statements about what could happen to the client if they do not see the error of their ways. These are statements like: '*If you don't watch out you may lose him*' or '*Be careful! – that will just make it worse*'. This is a type of negative fortune telling, whereas *reassuring*, also a form of fortune telling, tends to be more positive in focus although it is still a roadblock to empathic connection.

Prematurely giving advice, making suggestions or providing solutions

Statements that give advice or make suggestions are usually based on the desire of the interviewer to fix the problem, residing in a belief that the client just needs some good ideas and they will be OK. If only life were so simple! Most clients need to be given time to explore issues before they can begin to think about their own approaches to a solution. Typically, advice often comes in the form of statements like: '*Why don't you … .*' '*How about trying … .*' or '*I suggest … .*' The impact of premature advice giving on clients can be to suggest that they and their issue are not being taken seriously. As well, with some clients, premature advice giving can lead to a kind of 'yes but' game where the interviewer offers advice and the client counters with a reason why it would/could not work – hence the 'yes but' process.

Persuading with logic, arguing or lecturing

This category of verbal block is based on the interviewer's belief that if only the client could see things clearly and logically then they would know how to manage. Statements of this kind often downgrade the importance of feelings. Here the interviewer acts as a *logical convincer* with statements like: '*Well just let's be sensible and look at things from another point of view*' or '*It seems that you just need to keep a cool head and think things through*'. This elevation of logical thinking processes over the other things that trouble and overwhelm clients often makes clients feel stupid.

Moralizing, telling clients what to do

This is also a type of advice giving, but this category takes the moral high ground and informs the client about how they *ought* to behave, think or feel. It may be preceded by the interviewer saying: '*Well I don't want to tell you how to behave, but I think you should …*' or '*I think you know what you should do …*' There is a strong element of criticism in these moralizing statements and their impact on vulnerable clients is often to make them feel like failures in life.

Disagreeing, judging, criticizing or blaming

These responses are seriously non-reflective and come fairly directly out of the interviewer's belief system. These are negative statements such as *'I wonder if you're not just being weak'*, or *'Your attitude to study has got you into a real mess'*. These also involve telling clients what to think or disagreeing with the client's view point as in *'Well I don't think you really believe that ...'* which often means 'I don't believe that'. The client may visibly shrivel in the face of these heavy blocks to the empathic communication process.

Agreeing, approving or praising

Empty agreeing or approving statements discourage the client from expressing honest feelings or beliefs. As well, praise not based on a realistic appreciation of the client's coping skills that may come as the professional relationship develops, is false and lacking in genuineness. For example a statement like: *'I know you are a really nice person and would not want to hurt her'* said to a woman who is struggling to discuss her aggressive feelings toward an elderly and difficult parent she is caring for, robs the client of encouragement to continue and acts as a real block to her honest sharing.

Shaming, ridiculing or labelling

Statements in this category attempt to control or manipulate clients by pointing out what the interviewer considers they have done wrong. Labelling is probably something everyone does at an internal level although not vocalizing these ideas limits their direct impact. Shaming, as in saying things like *'A person your age should know how to budget'* or *'A good mother does not hit her child'* is a big roadblock to a client feeling accepted. Likewise making fun of, ridiculing or labelling clients clearly has no place in the competent interviewer's response repertoire.

Interpreting or analysing

This is a really tempting aspect of interviewer style, partly because many attracted to human service work often have a natural tendency to seek deeper meanings about people's motivations and personality problems. As well, many clients may expect it. So the fates conspire to lead practitioners into this quagmire of analysis and interpretation where they make up stories about clients' *real* reasons for doing things, their undeclared motivations and secret desires – often on the basis of minimal information. For example, early in the interview a worker says, *'It seems to me that your adult relationships are all reflections of your hostile feelings towards your father'*. Professional power may stifle the client's opposition to these clever ideas, even though they feel confused, belittled and manipulated by them.

Reassuring, sympathizing or consoling

This is another natural error in interviewing. Whereas many interviewers know it is not done to judge, to moralize or even to interpret, pieces of reassurance or sympathy trip so lightly off the interviewer's tongue. *'I am sure it will not be as bad as you fear'*, *'I know you will cope really well'* or *'Never mind, you poor thing – it will be alright'* may seem like sweet things to say. However, their impact is to block and divert the client from facing up to the demands of their life and may stop them from being honest about the real circumstances in their lives in the interview setting.

Questioning or probing

Probing and questioning do have a place in a well-managed interview but it is necessary to understand their proper uses and to understand that these *do not* show empathic understanding. Probes *direct* or *divert* the client and sometimes this is a deliberate tactic to keep clients on focus or to move them along when needed. Often however questions just happen without any real intention on the part of the interviewer – just to fill a void or for something to say – and these questions poke and prod clients to tell the interviewer things they *think* they need to know. Being a *deliberate* and *intentional* user of questions however is part of professional interviewing competence – and this is discussed later.

Withdrawing, distracting, humouring or changing the subject

Most commonly, this category of roadblock is about trying to take the heat off an interviewing situation. It often consists of the practitioner talking about themselves or changing the subject to happier things to distract the client. *'Well I like swimming – have your tried the new pool yet?'* to a client who has been talking about their struggle with weight and embarrassment about it. As clients often feel stopped from further exploration by these tactics, the distraction impact is strong. Ivey and

Ivey (2008, p. 51) mention the deliberate application of 'non–attention' for positive purposes such as to close down a passage of client talk that is going nowhere but this tactic requires professional judgement.

It is not uncommon for inexperienced interviewers to combine several 'roadblocks' in the same statement to a client. For example, with a client who has shared their struggle and despair in dealing with the pressure of their obligation to both work and family, the practitioner may start with a blocking order *'Don't feel like that!'*, add a reassurance *'I'm sure you will manage just fine'*, move on with a distracting probe *'Now tell me about your family'* and then later add an advice-riddled, moralizing closed question *'Are you really planning to keep working even with the current problems in the family?'* By this point the client's head is reeling and she has probably received a strong message that the practitioner is not interested in her feelings or concerns and what's more does not approve of her.

The best kind of empathic response is the *paraphrase*, the structure of which is discussed in the next chapter. Paraphrases contain reflections about how the client *feels* about *what is happening to or around them* and maybe *how the client behaves within this situation*. These elements, combined meaningfully within a grammatically accurate response with causal links between the components, show clients they have been understood and assist them to understand their feelings, the circumstances of their life and their part in contributing to these through their own behaviour.

ROADBLOCKS TO EMPATHY

1. Ordering, directing and commanding
2. Warning, cautioning and threatening
3. Giving premature advice, suggestions or solutions
4. Persuading with logic, arguing and lecturing
5. Moralizing, telling clients what to do
6. Disagreeing, judging, criticizing and blaming
7. Agreeing, approving or praising
8. Shaming, ridiculing and labelling
9. Interpreting and analysing
10. Reassuring, sympathizing or consoling
11. Inappropriately questioning and probing
12. Distracting, humouring, withdrawing or changing subject inappropriately

CHAPTER OVERVIEW

This chapter has defined the processes involved in establishing a clear understanding of the client's world and establishing a basis of trust, by accepting the
client's view of their current experiences and their feelings about these. This
approach is the cornerstone of effective practice when established especially
when it is combined with a consistent nonverbal attentiveness. Verbal and nonverbal skills build an empathic structure that facilitates the progression of
clients' understanding of self over time. Roadblocks to an empathic approach
were defined and the particular challenges involved when an interpreter is part
of the interview process were discussed briefly. By this point it is hoped that
the reader has a clear understanding of the skills required in effectively managing an interview and to define the key features of reflective responding. The
book now moves on to look at the structure and purpose of the empathic
paraphrase as a hallmark of effective responding.

CHAPTER 3

Paraphrasing as the Foundation of Effective Responding

The initial stage of an effective interview provides clients with consistent encouragement to describe their current situations from within their own frame of reference – their understandings, perceptions, feelings, experiences and values. Whatever the setting or purpose of an interview, the interviewer needs to establish rapport and provide reassurance to clients that their interests are important. The use of reflective empathy, as discussed to some extent in the last chapter, is most appropriate to achieve these purposes. All reflective skills are based on effective and focused attending, observing and listening in that they closely follow what the client expresses both verbally and nonverbally. Consistent attention to emotional and other experiential elements in the client's world enables interviewers to stay within the client's frame of reference rather than basing responses on own beliefs and needs. This chapter explains the structure and purpose of the paraphrase, the most essential type of response consistently employed by competent interviewers. Principles of intentionality enable the competent interviewer to use particular skills to achieve particular aims.

Reflective components of the paraphrase

Egan (2007, p. 102) refers to this understanding of elements of the client's world as 'sharing empathic highlights' – a recasting of his previous emphasis on paraphrasing, a term, along with 'restatement', he now avoids using. I still find paraphrasing a useful term to encapsulate a particular type of response. I consider a paraphrase is an attempt to combine, in a coherent and meaningful sentence, reflections about the clients' feelings, the situations and/or their behavioural responses to it. These components form the basis of all empathic responses in their own right. At times the practitioner may only pick up on *feelings* expressed by the client – a feeling reflection. At other times descriptions of occurrences in aspects of their life – which I refer to as the *situation* – seem to be most important to the client. Other times what clients think, decide or do about these situations in their lives will be the focus of a response – and this is termed the *behaviour* component.

For the sake of classifying or identifying responses, in this book I refer to these three components **when used on their own** as *reflections* – with the terms (feeling, situation or behaviour) added to show the particular focus. Any two *reflections* put together meaningfully are considered to make a paraphrase. Thus a reflection of *feeling*, 'You feel overwhelmed' linked with a reflection of *situation* 'three difficult assignments are all due this week' linked by 'because' becomes a paraphrase – i.e. 'You feel overwhelmed because three difficult assignments are all due this week' (Paraphrase with *feeling* and *situation*).

It is important to discriminate between these three components – of *feeling*, *situation* and *behaviour*. The ability to discriminate between the different foci of responses is directly linked to the interviewer's ability to produce intentional and purposeful responses in the interviewing setting. In turn, the ability to discriminate, between a reflection of feeling, situation and behaviour or between closed and open probes, means effective and purposeful responses are made in practice. This all relates to the important concept of intentionality in interviewing (Ivey and Ivey 2003, pp. 17–22) and the emphasis on the interviewer as a deliberate and self-directed professional. I firmly believe that understanding the nature of verbal responses and the ability to focus these on the three different elements in the client's narrative – the feelings, situations and behaviours – is central to responding empathically to the client.

Reflection of feeling

A reflection of feeling is an interviewer response which acknowledges the emotional state or affect of the client. It is a *reflection* of the client's emotional experience, sourced from their story. Sources of information about feelings are various. Clients express their feelings verbally (that is the client may actually say, 'I feel angry' or 'I feel really pleased'). They also express emotions nonverbally through complex displays of sighs, voice tones, facial expressions, gestures, physiological phenomenon such as blushing, perspiring or trembling and other body movements and posture changes. Sometimes feelings may not be readily displayed through these means, but are able to be read by the interviewer from the descriptions of events as narrated by the client. The basic format of a feeling reflection is 'You feel (feeling/emotion word)'– as in 'You feel really confident'. Feeling reflections can be expressed more creatively too, as in 'I sense your deep disappointment there' or 'I can hear you are boiling with anger'. The test of a response as a feeling reflection is its focus on the current *emotions* or *affect* of the client. Emotions or feelings are an important aspect of reflective work. Effectiveness in this area rests on the ability of the interviewer to observe the client's nonverbal reactions and empathically consider the client's situation. Ivey and Ivey (2008) devote a whole chapter to the importance of working with the emotional content of client's experiences. Empathic responses that pay attention to client's feelings, perceptions and experiences encourage clients to explore life issues more deeply.

Immediacy as a quality of feeling reflections

It can be important to differentiate between feelings that are part of the client's *past* experience and feelings that are *immediate* and being experienced as the client speaks to the interviewer. This is an important distinction, as feelings that are part of a past situation are really just that – in the past. Feelings are part of the client's current narration of the story in the here and now and so are experienced in the present moment of the interview. This means the immediate emotions need to be recognized. As an example, in responding to a client who is telling the interviewer about how they lost their cool, became really angry and punched someone, it is important to recognize how this person feels in the present as they tell this tale. It is possible they are no longer 'angry', a strong and 'out-there' emotion that is active and outwardly directed, but that now they feel ashamed, a quieter, more inwardly directed emotion. This reading of the immediate feeling is obtained through noticing the client's facial expressions, voice tone and so on as they speak. The empathic value of acknowledging feelings is magnified when immediate or here and now emotions are attended to in the interviewer's responses.

The nature of feelings

Feelings can be categorized into broad families or groups and these are useful as some sort of early classification of clients' emotions as they narrate their story. These categories can be loosely called *mad, sad, bad, glad* and *afraid*.

These five categories move some distance towards catching the range of emotions that clients express. Human feelings are complex however and individually unique. The hunt for the right emotional word for a particular client's feeling in a particular moment is a constant one and categories such as these suggested provide only limited guidance in this task.

CATEGORIES OF FEELINGS

The mad category of feelings is *active* and *outwardly directed negatively towards other people*, such as irritation, resentment, anger and fury. Clients often describe these feelings as being caused by others' aggravation, bad behaviour and so on.

The sad feelings are *inactive* and *down*, in a category of emotions that are largely *self-directed*, related to sadness, grief, loss and depression and other low levels of affect such as boredom. Clients often describe these feelings as descending on them from out there or above. Sometimes these are described as being caused by other people's behaviour.

The bad category are *active* in they are self-directed impulses and are *down* in focus in that are largely self-critical related to shame, embarrassment, guilt and similar emotions. These are fed strongly by negative self-talk often about self-blame and sometimes by other people's criticism and rejection.

The *glad* category – a rather neglected one in the history of the helping professions – is '*up*' in mood and actively optimistic about the *self or others* with feelings of happiness, pride, love, affection, relief and other positive feelings.

The *afraid* category involves *outwardly looking* feelings but with some sense of recoil, especially when associated with feelings like horror, fear and terror. Some feelings in this category are less vivid however and include worry, anxiety, fear and stress. These too can be seen as caused by events or other people's behaviour but can be fed by self-talk that catastrophizes and imagines the worst.

Expanding vocabularies to accurately acknowledge clients' feelings

Even if interviewers 'read' the emotion well, it can be difficult to locate the right words to convey understanding of a client's emotional state. Many people lack a good emotional vocabulary – a product of low levels of emotional courtesy or attention to feelings in some societies. As well, in some cultures non-recognition or low attention to emotions is a gender issue. Sometimes people's feelings are dismissed as messy, untidy things.

Improving one's alertness to emotions is important, but so is extending the range of words available to describe what is noticed. It can be good practice to search for feeling words and terms when there is no pressure to respond, such as while watching a TV show or a film, or observing people's interactions in public spaces such as on buses and trains or in cafes. In all these situations, it is possible to look for a range of expressed emotions and to locate words to describe these in a search for greater vocabulary richness. In trying to improve one's range of feeling words, it may be useful to keep an *emotions journal* to work on building up a comprehensive list of feeling words and terms. For those developing their interviewing expertise, such exercises may contribute to the broadening and widening of a vocabulary of words and terms about emotional experiences and states. Cournoyer (2000, pp. 423–428) may be a useful resource here in composing such a list, in that he suggests a wild and wide variety of words to refer to clients' feelings or emotions.

It is important to ensure the word *feel* is employed to focus on emotions. Sometimes by using words loosely such as in 'You feel that money is tight', might suggest feelings are being discussed even though this is not a feeling reflection. The word *feel* here really means *think* or *believe* and so it is actually a reflection of *situation – not feeling*. It is important to learn to be quite selective about using the word 'feel' to refer only to emotional states, as this will help to educate clients about this important aspect of their experiences in life and in time to discriminate more carefully between their feelings and what they do with these – that is their behaviour.

Being attentive to people's feelings is also a matter of professional sensitivity and courtesy. Clients feel affirmed and supported by practitioners who notice and speak about feelings. In general then, a *feeling reflection* is a response focusing on a here-and-now or immediate emotion or affect being experienced or expressed by the client as they narrate their story. The feeling reflection in its simplest form looks like this: 'You feel relieved' and the formula is this: 'You feel/are feeling + emotion/ feeling (e.g. relieved, dismayed, terrified or irritated'). More colloquial expression as mentioned previously often means feeling reflections vary in their expression such as in: 'You seem to be very jumpy' or 'You are all up in the air'. Phrases such as these can catch emotional states quite well. Consistent use of reflections of the client's current emotions in language they understand shows the interviewer is working hard to notice the signs of these feeling states and recognizes the importance of these in the client's story. Ivey and Ivey (2003, pp. 148–175) provide a thorough review of other perspectives on reflecting feelings and emphasize the feeling reflection as one of the most important aspects of empathic responding.

Following on the next few pages are some lists of 'feeling' words to help to extend vocabularies. Look over these and see if there are other feeling words you can add that belong in some of these categories related to the sad, mad, bad, afraid and glad – as mentioned previously.

Feeling word lists

This list is NOT the definitive list – and there are many others able to be added. Also note some feeling words seem to work across related categories.

FEELING WORDS

SAD	HURT	ANGRY	FURIOUS
tearful	disappointed	mad	livid
sorrowful	tormented	annoyed	enraged
pained	deprived	hostile	worked up
grieving	pained	insulted	mad
anguished	tortured	indignant	bad
desolated	rejected	irritated	incensed
desperate	injured	upset	furious
pessimistic	offended	offended	in a stew
unhappy	afflicted	bitter	vehement
lonely	crushed	resentful	outraged
mournful	victimized	frustrated	
dejected	humiliated	cross	fuming
heartbroken	wronged	cold	infuriated
dismayed	alienated	heated	gnashing your teeth

ASHAMED	UNCERTAIN/ UNCLEAR	AFRAID	OVERPOWERED
lousy	upset	fearful	tortured
disappointed	guilty	terrified	tormented
discouraged	uncertain	scared	deprived
ashamed	indecisive	anxious	pained

Continued

FEELING WORDS (Continued)

ASHAMED	UNCERTAIN/ UNCLEAR	AFRAID	OVERPOWERED
powerless	perplexed	alarmed	alienated
diminished	hesitant	frightened	rejected
miserable	ashamed	panicky	injured
terrible	indecisive	stunned	offended
dismal	unsure	hesitant	afflicted
bad	uneasy	worried	overwhelmed
pessimistic	disillusioned	terrorized	victimized
sad	sorry	indespair	beaten
burdened	doubtful	nervous	trounced
distressed	useless	shaky	threatened
mortified	distrustful	vulnerable	paralysed
humiliated	wary	suspicious	crushed
embarrassed	suspicious		

OPEN	HAPPY	ALIVE	CALM
understanding	great	playful	blessed
clear	elated	courageous	peaceful
reliable	joyous	energetic	at ease
easy	jubilant	liberated	comfortable
amazed	fortunate	optimistic	pleased
free	delighted	impulsive	bright
sympathetic	overjoyed	free	clever
interested	gleeful	frisky	content
satisfied	thankful	animated	quiet
receptive	festive	spirited	certain
accepting	ecstatic	thrilled	relaxed
kind	glad	wonderful	serene
	cheerful	excited	free and easy
	merry		

LOVING	INTERESTED	POSITIVE	STRONG
loving	concerned	eager	secure
considerate	affected	keen	free
affectionate	fascinated	earnest	sure
sensitive	intrigued	intent	certain
tender	absorbed	hopeful	independent
devoted	inquisitive	inspired	unique
attracted	nosy	determined	dynamic
passionate	snoopy	encouraged	tenacious

Continued

FEELING WORDS   (Continued)

LOVING	INTERESTED	POSITIVE	STRONG
admiring	engrossed	enthusiastic	hardy
warm	curious	daring	resilient
touched	drawn toward	challenged	brave
sympathetic	intent	reassured	bold
close	focused	lucky	optimistic
	excited	confident	powerful
			in charge

Reflection of situation

This is about reflecting the client's perceptions of what has *happened to them* or what they believe *others have done to them* or to others, e.g. *'Study has gone really well this year'*, or *'She ignored you completely'*. Being able to capture in a few meaningful words what has been happening to clients is the central purpose of the *situation* component. Situations described by the client in the interview setting are usually surrounded by the feelings that were part of them at the time and are still alive in the client's mind. Feelings and situations are often mixed up in the client's perceptions and it may be hard for them to differentiate these. I think it is essential to appreciate these as different aspects of the client's story in preparing clients to gradually understand what they are responsible for and may wish to change and what remains beyond their power to influence.

In the following statement, the client probably has a range of feelings surrounding what is happening. 'It's been a hard run. When my wife got sick I thought it would only be for a week that I would need to stay home to look after the baby. But it has gone on – she's had tests but they can't seem get to the bottom of it. I have used up all my leave and I need to get back to work but I can't really leave her with the care of the baby all day. I am feeling a bit frantic'.

There would be worry and anxiety because *his wife's illness is going on and remains unclear*. There is high anxiety because *his leave is used up and* it is likely he will not be paid unless he goes back to work. But he feels afraid – and as he says frantic – because *the baby needs looking after* as does his wife and *his job and the family's livelihood will be jeopardized soon*. The situations (or experiences) are often described by clients as *happening to them* – sometimes through other people's agency or just life or bad luck! These are often described as externalized views of their world – happenings for which clients do not see themselves as responsible. In this example, his wife is sick, the baby needs caring for, his leave is all gone, his job may be at risk – all things that have happened to him and he does not see that he made them happen. When feelings seem fairly clear and the situations are described as external phenomena, then paraphrases containing these elements (feelings and situations) will help the client feel supported rather than blamed and to further extend the narrative.

As discussion goes on and the client's narrative widens and deepens, it may be appropriate to focus on solutions, if any are to be found. If so, the client needs to begin to focus on what he *is responsible for* or *can influence* because those are the only things that he can change. Clients and interviewers may need to work especially hard to locate and understand these aspects termed *behaviours*, which include phrases about the client's own *actions or reactions* to these situations.

Reflection of behaviour

This reflective component picks up and reinforces clients' descriptions about their own current pieces of behaviours or reactions in the situation (what they do, and what they are thinking about doing). Behaviours are things **the client** *enacts in some way* – sometimes towards other people or objects, sometimes to self maybe as internal cognitive processes. As a demonstration of this focus, *verbs* or *doing* words are the essential element in a behaviour reflection. So a *client* acts or behaves towards other people or things e.g. '*You explained to your boss* you can't keep going on like this' or '*You asked him* for some extra leave'. Usually the behaviour reflection also begins with 'you', because here the worker is attempting to name *the client's behaviours* towards others or factors in the situation *e.g. 'You made an appointment with the bank manager to ask for a loan'.*

It is important to see these behaviours as current aspects of what the client is doing – and *not* focus them on what the client is *not doing* or *can't do* – as this is usually of little value. For example if a client wishes to lose weight, it is more useful to focus on a goal related to 'eating three small meals a day comprising healthy foods and walking for 20 minutes each day' – and not on 'avoiding buying candy bars and staying away from TV watching'. Reflecting clients' dysfunctional behaviour, which they need to stop, can be quite confronting to them anyway – especially if this is before a basis of trust is established between the client and practitioner. If these behaviours need to be focused on – rather than more coping and positive behaviours – it is essential to wait until a shared understanding about feelings and situations is established before taking the focus onto negative or dysfunctional client behaviours. This is especially so if these acts are harmful to others or self. In all cases, it is important to think of the behaviour components as describing pieces of behaviour that could be recorded on a video if it was running and following the client around. Some of what would be recorded might be positive things or dysfunctional things and some things would not be recorded because they happen inside the client's head and we only gain insight into these when the client tells us about them. Behaviour reflections focus on both *external* and *internal* behaviours.

Reflections of behaviour about external acts usually focus on things the client is doing/has done that others could observe and notice in some way if they were present. *Internal* behaviours – cognitive processes that happen on the inside, or behaviours directed at the self – are less clear to others. Internal processes include self-talk – e.g. '*You keep telling yourself "he hates me"*' or '*You are going over and over in your head what happened*'. These processes of internal dialogue usually concern the client's self-estimations or other cognitive processes. In the following small case it can be seen how easy it is to miss the internal dialogue issues.

> **Client**: I've been off work now for over three months and I am starting to get anxious about not moving on a bit. There's a sense of being in a vacuum – and not making any progress on this rotten depression – where I sometimes find myself saying I can't keep this going – and then it gets pretty black in my head.
>
> **Practitioner**: '*You feel a bit discouraged*', *which* is a reflection of feeling but seems very low key and leaves out what is happening inside the client's head. A paraphrase like '*You sometimes tell yourself it's not worth the effort and then you start to feel scared*' makes a better attempt to focus on the internal behaviour – what is happening inside the client's head as well as linking this to a more appropriate feeling reflection.

Self-directed processes or actions may also have visible elements – but these are often symbolic of other things going on inside the client's thoughts and through self-talk. For example, '*You stayed in bed all day*' may be attached to feelings of hopelessness and negative or self-critical self-talk. Likewise, '*You got drunk each night this week*' or '*You broke your diet and ate the whole tub of ice cream'* are sometimes external indicators of internal dialogue and other cognitions that need to be uncovered in further exploration with the client. It is important to attend to all these different aspects of the client's behaviours – external, internal and self-directed – to build up a well-rounded view of what the client is doing so as to structure paraphrases that encompass and link important features of the client's inner world.

Interpretive or judgemental ways of naming socially negative or dysfunctional behaviours – whether external or internal in nature – are to be avoided. For example, it is not a good idea to say, 'I think you might be transferring your aggro to the kids rather than facing up to your marriage problems'. A more positive slant on the client's behaviour may encourage them to feel supported and able to focus on what is working well for them, rather than only on the problems and disasters in life. A paraphrase like 'You feel pleased, because although the kids are a handful, you keep your temper most of the time', may encourage this direction.

Linking components to make a paraphrase

A response is termed a paraphrase when it combines two, or all three, of the previous components, i.e. reflections of *feelings*, *situations* and *behaviours*, in a coherent sentence. As an example 'You feel *relieved* (feeling) because *Jenny passed all her subjects* (situation) and *you rewarded her by making a special dinner to celebrate it'* (behaviour). Another combination of *reflections* produces the following paraphrase: 'I sense you *feel really pleased* (f), because *study is really important in your life* (s) and *you are working hard and getting good results'* (b).

An effective paraphrase grasps the importance of key issues and links them in a coherent, reflective statement that is concise and accurate. Usually it is preferable to use 'own words' to attain this concise and accurate response. Reiterating or 'parroting' what the client says is to be avoided as this is not paraphrasing. Paraphrasing requires an overview of a client's situation. Until this is clear – usually requiring some period of interaction between the interviewer and the client – then single reflections of feeling or situation may be all that is possible. A paraphrase is deeper in focus than a reflection as it attends to the links between clients' feelings, situations and behaviours but the client narrative needs to deepen too to provide the context for these. Egan refers to the 'key experiences and behaviours' as giving rise to 'clients' feelings, emotions and moods' (2007, p. 107). A well-constructed paraphrase shows these causal links.

Examples of paraphrases

Note that elements such as the feeling and situation need to be causally linked to each other – and this link is often shown with the use of the word 'because' as in the following: *'You are furious (f) because you asked her to bring the books to class (b), but she let you down by not showing up' (s).* In this example the feeling (of fury) is *causally linked* to the situation but it is also relevant to the behaviour component as it is the client's 'asking' that meant the 'not showing up' resulted in fury.

The following client is narrating her difficulties in financial management: *'I feel bad about how I manage my finances. I get a reasonable salary but I also have a lot of bills and a mortgage to keep going. I spend more than I should though and I sometimes leave paying bills to the last minute and then can't afford to pay them. Then to help me forget about it all I go shopping and have a real spend up – so I have more bills the next month! Dumb eh?'*

Situation elements here include the good salary, financial pressures and lots of bills. The behaviour elements are about the client leaving bill paying to last or spending money to avoid it all and the feeling elements include anxiety (about financial pressures, unpaid bills) and shame (about avoiding/spending/poor financial management).

Now as mentioned a single paraphrase cannot catch *everything* nor is it meant to be *perfect* but it does need to focus on central aspects of the client's narrative. So a paraphrase for the previous example could look something like: *'You feel ashamed because despite your good salary you rarely pay your bills on time'.* This one has **feeling** and **behaviour** components causally linked, but it *is* fairly negative. It might be preferable, therefore, especially early on in the interview to focus more on **situational** elements, such as *'You feel anxious because the financial pressures seem unrelenting'.* This is by way of suggesting that there is often no *perfect* paraphrase able to be derived from most clients' narratives and it is about estimating, from the client's expression as well as general presentation and nonverbal behaviour, what seems best to focus on. Following are some client statements and suggested elements in each of the three categories that can comprise paraphrases – *feeling*, *situation* and *behaviour*.

My boss is really out of control – he shouts at us, swears and even pushes some of the girls around physically sometimes. I try to stay out of his way. I feel like letting him know what I think of him but he might sack me if I did. So I don't say anything – I just duck or hide – but then I feel like a coward – and he keeps getting away with it!

Feeling: ashamed, frightened;

Situation: boss is acting abusively; he has the power to sack you;

Behaviour: you do nothing to intervene, you keep your head down.

Putting these components together makes a paraphrase looking like this: 'You do nothing to intervene (b) when the boss behaves abusively (s) and you feel a bit ashamed (f) but because you feel frightened (f) he could sack you (s), you just keep your head down (b).' In this long and complex response, which attempts to catch all aspects, the causal links are apparent between the feelings, situations and behavioural elements – the shame about his behaviour and his fear about the boss's possible reaction.

Here are some other client statements broken down into words related to the three categories:

I'm finding study so hard since I came back. I feel so tired looking after the baby and trying to get in to class on time. I am only going to Uni Monday to Wednesday – but I get nothing much done in my days off because of the baby. I am scared because all my assignments are due soon. But I keep putting off making a start on them – just stare at the books – can't seem to get focused.

Feeling (f): anxious

Situation (s): the assignments need attention

Behaviour (b): you put most of your energy into looking after the baby

'You put most of your energy into looking after the baby and you feel anxious because the assignments now need attention.'

I have stopped going to those training sessions – so thought I'd let you know. I don't really think I need them anyway – grooming and all that stuff about presenting well for job interviews – waste of time. Nobody ever gives me an interview anyway as they usually say the job is filled or something like that when I ring up. I think it's all a bit pointless.

Feeling (f): disheartened

Situation (s): nobody has offered you an interview

Behaviour (b): you are telling yourself it's all useless

'You feel disheartened and you are telling yourself it's all useless because no one has offered you an interview'.

Here the feeling is causally linked to both the situation and his own internal behaviour.

I have messed up my life a bit – broke up with my girlfriend, failed my first year at Uni and I owe parking fines I can't afford to pay. So, I am going to do a flit – I been thinking that I need a holiday anyway – somewhere warm – I can go on the dole for a while and when I come back – well I'll face it all then.

Feeling (f): disillusioned
Situation (s): finances, study and relationships have all gone wrong
Behaviour (b): you are telling yourself it is better to just cut loose
'You feel disillusioned because finances, study and relationships have all gone wrong and you are telling yourself it's better to cut loose for a while'.

As you read this example, I wonder how many of you wanted to focus on his "irresponsible" attitudes. It is tempting, but that might need to wait until more of the story comes out. In the example, the externalized view of the situation and the neutral focus on the client's internal behaviour ascribes no real blame or responsibility and provides room for further exploration.

Order of components in a paraphrase

There is no right order in which the components of paraphrase should appear and consequently in the preceding examples, sometimes this varies. There is some logic however to placing the feeling element in the lead position. Feelings are both very important and sometimes easier to locate in the narrative and in the client's nonverbal behaviour. Placing feelings first in the paraphrase ensures these are noticed by the client. Sometimes, however, the situation component might be put first in a paraphrase or even the behaviour component. For instance, in the last example, the response could be structured thus: '*You are telling yourself it's better to just to cut loose (b) because finances and relationships have all gone wrong (s) and you feel disillusioned (f)*'.

However, the order of the components can alter the emphasis or overall meaning so it is not inconsequential. Sometimes the things said first may be related to the clearest or strongest aspects of the client's expression and the client may then pick up on these things and go on before the response is fully expressed. This may mean other elements do not get expressed at all sometimes, leading to incomplete paraphrases (or only reflections) being offered. This also means the connections between aspects of clients' worlds – like how the feelings are related to situations *and* to how they behave – may not be made. If this keeps happening sometimes it is worth asking the client to let you construct a complete paraphrase as they may be missing out on features that would help them put things together better and to feel more deeply understood by the interviewer.

Whenever possible, interviewers should take the time to consider the component parts and structure of paraphrases and to ensure that responses contain at least two elements, expressed with a causal link. This gradually builds a picture of the relationships between feelings and situations and in time makes it possible for the behavioural reactions to be clearer for the client to see. In time this also allows both client and the interviewer to gain a clearer picture of the overall state of affairs as described in the client's narrative.

It is emphasized then that potent paraphrases contain clearly expressed components focused on feelings, situations and behaviours and that these elements are linked *causally*. This means that the feeling is described as being produced or flowing out of the situation and/or behaviour and ideally the situation and behaviour are linked too. In considering the preceding examples, recall that the feeling is sometimes linked to the overall combination of situational and behavioural elements. Sometimes however, the feeling is clearly linked to *only* the situation or to their behaviour, so that where it is placed is more important. From the example about the person feeling disheartened because no one has offered them an interview, the feeling is linked to the situation but the behaviour element derives from and is linked with the feeling too.

In summary then, well-linked paraphrases that consistently include all three elements provide the best basis for effective exploration of the client's current world and for goal work later on in the process, as discussed in further chapters. This is because a well-constructed paraphrase, with causally linked components of feeling, situation and behaviour, helps clients to understand the difference *and* the relationships between their own feelings, the situations and their own behaviours or actions – and this is part of the education of the client during the first phase of interviewing. But for this to occur within the interviewing process, the interviewer needs to master the ability to differentiate clearly between feelings, situations and behaviours and to construct responses that focus on these elements in a purposeful and deliberate way.

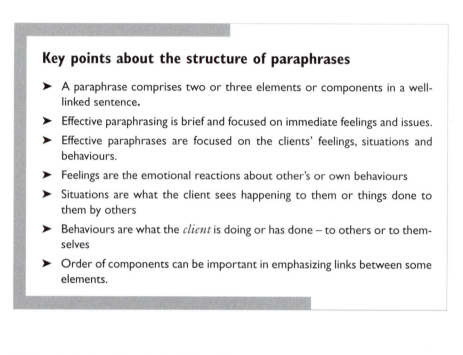

Key points about the structure of paraphrases

➤ A paraphrase comprises two or three elements or components in a well-linked sentence.

➤ Effective paraphrasing is brief and focused on immediate feelings and issues.

➤ Effective paraphrases are focused on the clients' feelings, situations and behaviours.

➤ Feelings are the emotional reactions about other's or own behaviours

➤ Situations are what the client sees happening to them or things done to them by others

➤ Behaviours are what the *client* is doing or has done – to others or to themselves

➤ Order of components can be important in emphasizing links between some elements.

Ways to help clients to identify and link feelings, situations and behaviours

It can be difficult for clients to distinguish own thoughts, feelings and actions in their narrative as these are often mixed up in the client's mind. Sometimes a flip-chart or white-board may be a useful prop during the interview, providing a visual means of tracking and noting the client's feelings, perceptions about what has happened (the situation) and what they are doing in it (their behaviours).

Self-talk and internal behaviours

As mentioned previously, behavioural elements of paraphrases can refer to *externally expressed* behaviours of the client – things that are visible, audible and able to be noticed by others in the situation e.g. 'You yelled at the kids' or 'You told him to get out'. In contrast, some behaviour is much more *internal*. Compared with externalized behaviours, these internal processes are not directly observable to other people and the interviewer needs to gain access to these through the client's narrative and insight into their self-talk to fully understand the complexity of the client's internal world. These include a range of cognitive functions including self-talk or repetitive thoughts that may have an obsessive status in some clients' minds. Sometimes observable behaviours – emanating from the internal processes such as acts of self-abuse or other observable behaviours – have a kind of symbolic nature representing internal struggles. These may be misunderstood unless this symbolism is appreciated. For example, alcohol overuse may be a symbol of a client's inner struggles with self-esteem anxiety and so on. There are always important distinctions to be made between what happens inside clients' heads, what happens at more observable levels and the relationship between these.

Separating feelings from situations/behaviours

Clients sometimes need help in seeing this linkage however as they may have feelings, situations and behaviours all mixed up in their perceptions as expressed in their narrative. Imagine an interview where the client is describing some domestic events where they lost their temper. The interviewer is trying to help them to see the difference between feeling angry and behaving aggressively. The interviewer says '*Tell me what happens when you get angry*'. Client says, '*What happens? – well what I do is – well, I just get angry*'. The interviewer indicates that this is now a feeling being discussed by saying '*You feel angry*' (feeling reflection) and writing 'angry' under a heading 'Feelings' on a flip-chart or board. Feelings might need to be checked for immediacy – by asking how the client feels *now* in discussing things with the interviewer. This process may go something like this: '*You say you felt angry. What's the feeling right now talking with me about this?*' Here the client may say – '*Well – a bit uncomfortable I guess*'. If so, that is put on the board too under the 'Feelings' heading. On the other hand, clients may not be able to answer this if it is not clear to them – and may just shrug and not say anything else.

The interviewer probes to get the client to describe the behaviour as separate from feelings: '*Let's talk about what you do when you feel angry*' (open probe re behaviour) client says: '*Well I get angry at the kids, don't I – like, they never do as they are told – and so there is some yelling I guess and then maybe one of them cops a smack or whatever*'. Note the continued confusion between feeling and other elements. Also note the externalized expression of these behaviours as things that 'just happen'. Other people such as 'the kids' are the focus. The client's own behaviour is described in a disengaged way – 'there is some yelling' and 'one of them cops a smack'. This disengaged attitude towards own acts of aggression and where others are described as deserving what happens can be typical of abusive patterns in family settings.

However, from what the client says about behaviours, the interviewer writes some more words on the board – 'yelling' and 'smacking' under a 'Behaviour' or 'Action' heading. Then the interviewer formulates a response that combines these *feelings, situational elements* and *behaviours*, drawing lines between these words on the board, to emphasize their separate yet connected presence in the client's narrative. *'So when you feel angry* → *because the kids don't do as they are told* → *you express your anger by yelling at them and sometimes smacking one of them – is that it?'* Now the interviewer has included the client's *feelings* expressed quite separately from the clearly identified client's *behaviours* – with feeling, situation and behaviours carefully worded to encourage this distinction.

With the use of the words on the board, the interviewer stresses how the feelings are linked to situation e.g. *'You are angry'* because *'the kids disobey you'* and then how feelings are linked to behaviours *'When you feel angry, you may yell and hit them'*. Care is taken here to differentiate between angry *feelings* and what clients often think are feelings but which are actually *behaviours* (the aggressive yelling and hitting) which are all mixed up with the angry feelings. Without this distinction some clients may accept no responsibility for being able to control their own behaviours. They see their anger *and* aggressive acts as out of their own control and produced entirely by provocation by others. It is essential to avoid buying into any client's lack of responsibility for aggressive behaviours emanating from strong feelings and this is best done by helping them to see the difference and the linkages between feelings, situations and their own behaviours. At the same time, it is essential to note any of the client's positive behaviours. Clients are often struggling to manage stressful and demanding life situations and interviewers should affirm them for what they manage well and for their efforts in attempting to bring about a better set of circumstances for themselves and others for whom they care.

> ## Key points about focusing and linking components of paraphrases
>
> ➤ Effective paraphrases contain clearly expressed components or elements which are linked *causally* to assist clients to learn the difference between these
>
> ➤ Clients need help to distinguish own thoughts, feelings and actions in their narrative
>
> ➤ Use of a whiteboard may assist clients to understand the links between components
>
> ➤ Clients are only able to take charge of or control those things which they are able to identify as within their realm of responsibility

Strengths perspective in paraphrasing

In a journal article published in 1994, Dennis Saleebey wrote: 'Practice is the intersection where the meanings of the worker (theories), the client (stories and narratives) and culture (myths, rituals and themes) meet' (Saleebey 1994, p. 35). Ivey and Ivey (2003, p. 27) echo Saleebey's themes in their statement, 'It is not enough to listen; it is vital that positive strengths and assets be discovered as part of clients' stories'. These writers, along with others, such as Egan (2007) and De Jong and Berg (2008), emphasize the foundational importance of finding and working with positives in the client's behaviours and experiences as fully as possible. At times however, it is necessary to focus on difficult and unpleasant aspects of life with clients. The trick is to move things along in the direction of locating what the client is doing well or right in the situation as well as noting the down side. This entails listening to the full range of a client's experiences and feelings and using a reframing method if necessary to focus on the positive coping skills discernible within their narrative. The client's feelings may be strongly negative at times (angry, resentful, furious, hopeless) and the situation may be harsh (no money, no job, poor health, abusive partner). It seems sometimes that no amount of positive talk will change this for the better. But perhaps in the midst of this the client is engaging in some good coping behaviours (keeping their temper, following a healthy diet, using good budgeting skills, applying for jobs every week, going to 'managing abusive spouse' classes) and any such positives deserve to be noticed, talked about and affirmed.

De Jong and Berg (2008) see valuing the client's strategies and skills as much more central to building solutions than any advice from so-called experts, the professionals. So, asking clients what they have tried so far, what has worked best and what they have learned from their efforts, might be the place to start in locating the clients as 'the expert about their own lives' (De Jong and Berg 2008, pp. 18, 19) and identifying their coping strengths. This is quite different from a 'what's wrong?' focus, which erodes the client's self-esteem where diagnoses, advice and so-called 'solutions' emanate from the practitioner's frame of reference. Instead of focusing on problems or problem solving, (which suggest the client is abnormal or dysfunctional), strengths-focused practitioners actively look for and focus on the skills and strengths that the client has used in the past or is currently using to manage the pressures of life. It can be presumed that clients who have been dealing with difficult life circumstances have inevitably learnt many skills in managing the challenging aspects of their life in the present and the past. In focusing on the skills of clients, practitioners can work as fully as possible within clients' frames of reference, thereby promoting the self-esteem of clients as well as strengthening their expert status within their own lives.

A good paraphrase usually has *feeling*, *situation* and *behaviour* knitted together in a meaningful way. By incorporating a *strengths perspective* in a paraphrase, the interviewer also emphasizes the skills or coping abilities in the client's narrative – ways in which they are managing well in the face of adversity and not just what is going wrong or what they have failed at. As in all reflective responses, there is choice about what to focus on. It is worth aiming to finish all interview sessions with a sense of having increased clients' sense of self-esteem, with appropriate affirming and positive framing of their abilities and strengths.

To some, this may sound like Pollyanna reincarnate. Students sometimes complain that if a client comes into the agency with lots of problems, it is difficult to focus on positive things. It is true that clients seem very problem focused – as discussed in Chapter 1 – and may believe this is required client behaviour in an interview. As stated before, a strengths approach does not avoid discussing the harsh and difficult aspects of a client's situation. The primary focus of the worker should remain one of empathic listening and this means that, at times, the difficult bits of the client's world do come into focus. When many clients come along expecting the intraction to be problem focused, practitioners may also need to engage them in a gradual educational process before clients even see their own strengths. Overall then, the weight of effort in interviewing remains on the client's current perceptions but there may need to be gentle encouragement to focus on coping skills and to learn to see a more positive future. To achieve this, the interviewer must pay keen attention to the client's story – the views, perceptions, opinions, beliefs and feelings in their narrative – drawn out through the use of empathic reflections and paraphrases.

By now it should be clear that when a response is reflective, it is focused on *feelings, situation* and *behaviour.* When these are combined in a response it can be termed a *paraphrase.* Understanding this enables the interviewer to formulate appropriately empathic responses that pay attention to the client's strengths and coping skills.

Key points about strengths-focused paraphrasing

➤ Although interviewers need to gently encourage clients to take responsibility for own actions, clients should be affirmed for what they manage well within difficult situations

➤ It is important to listen to the full range of a client's experiences and feelings and to use a reframing method if necessary to focus on the positive coping skills

➤ Clients' self-esteem is increased by using appropriate affirming and positive framing of their abilities and strengths

Purposes of summaries

A summary is an attempt to pull together broader themes related to feelings, situations and behaviours from the client's narrative. Summaries are a good idea before moving to another issue or topic.

Summarizing at the end of interviews highlights the main issues, notes clients' achievements and can conclude the interaction. Summaries may look very similar to paraphrases at times, in that they often have feeling, situation and behaviour components, but they are different in purpose and intent. A summary is an attempt to mark a pause or ending and as such includes broader issues, overview points or clients' decisions. A paraphrase intends to encourage clients' further exploration and talk, whereas a summary attempts to close off an issue.

Often it is necessary to *signal* what the interviewer is intending with a summary because, being reflective in nature, a well-focused summary may encourage the client to keep on with the narrative. A summary may need to be preceded with a clear signal of intention as in this following example: 'OK – I'd like to see if I can pull all this together for you. You have told me about how you faced some challenges this year. The move to the city two months ago was a wrench, finding accommodation was hard, getting your finances sorted and enrolling at uni has been a struggle too – and very stressful. But you've settled in to a flat, made new friends and worked out your finances and your study program – and although you still miss your family lots you feel more hopeful now, about the move, your study and the future. I'd like to move on now if we can, to discuss how your finances are going'. Summaries can help to bring a client into a more settled point before moving them on to another area and are an essential tool in the process of managing the focus and direction of the interview as discussed in Chapter 5.

Key points about summaries

➤ A summary may mark a pause or an ending in the client's narrative

➤ Summaries include broad issues, key overview points or clients' decisions

➤ It may be advisable to *signal* what is intended with a summary to avoid eliciting further client narrative

CHAPTER OVERVIEW

This chapter has explained the structure and function of the paraphrase in terms of component parts and the causal links between these. Principles of intentionality were defined as essential to enabling the competent practitioner to apply different reflections of feeling, situation and behaviour, to combine these into paraphrases and to apply summaries for particular purposes in the interview. The strengths perspective has been revisited in this chapter to emphasize its essential place within most professional interaction in the human services. In addition, this chapter has emphasized the vital importance of seeing all empathic responses as purposively employed to achieve particular ends.

The book now progresses to the difficult aspects of deciding when and why to employ questions and other probes in interacting with clients within professional contexts.

CHAPTER 4

Prompting the Client and Recording the Interview

In beginning an interview, building the professional relationship and in establishing the initial focus, questions and other probes have limited application unless there is a need to focus, shift topics or deliberately refocus the client. Prompts, such as questions and probes, are not effective means to encourage clients to expand their narration. Yet, one of the commonest faults in many interviews is the overuse of questions and probes – motivated by the pressure to achieve aims and to gain what may be viewed as essential information. Added pressure may derive also from agency or other demands to retain and record information gained in the interview.

Kadushin and Kadushin (1997, pp. 244–248) see probing as having a particular use when the client is being either non-specific or incomplete in their description of an issue as does Egan (2007, pp. 126–127). In this sense they describe the probe or question as a prompting device to prise out extra information. This sounds coercive and I prefer to see the probe as a structural tool rather than an interrogative one. It is always more important to respond reflectively and to show interest in what has been said, rather than focusing on what has not yet been said. Questions and other probes should be reserved for deliberate and purposeful use and for achieving specific purposes.

Egan (2007, p. 124) warns that 'Helpers, especially novices and inept counsellors, tend to ask too many questions' and my own experiences lead me to concur with this view. Many students use questions badly, particularly when they encounter points of tension, silence or other tight spots in the professional interaction. Their worst use demonstrates low-level listening and rock bottom empathy, as in the following example:

> **Client**: I've been in this job for a few months. It is such hard work and I feel flat after finishing each week – so I get very tired. But as I need the money I just need to get used to the pace.
>
> **Worker**: How much do you earn a week?

The focus here is intrusive and does not pick up on other important aspects of the client's issues and none of the client's feelings. If this pattern persists, the client will begin to feel less and less like exploring feelings and ideas. Using frequent and badly directed questions and other probes limits the amount of free information the client volunteers. This also puts the interviewer in an uncomfortable role of driving the interview and thus constantly needing to think of what to ask next. Questions and other probes are best saved for times where there is a need to deliberately focus or move the client to another issue or point.

Causes of inappropriate probing

Unfortunately, when an interviewer feels under pressure – such as when the client is silent for a while, the conversation grinds to a halt, or there is a difficult passage where the situation becomes uncomfortable – these are likely to be the times when questions happen. The least justifiable yet most frequent use of probes and questions occurs when the interviewer cannot think of what else to say – an occasion when instead silence is highly recommended. It is also the case that many interviewers overuse questioning without even being conscious of doing so. Interrogating the client through questioning sometimes springs from the interviewer's need to know something, but more often questions just pop out, often because the worker does not know what to say next.

Some interviewers use many questions quite deliberately however, because they believe this will keep the client talking as though this alone is the marker of an interview's success. As well, interviewers may believe that questions and other probes are necessary to achieve the purposes of the interview, when these exist, or to manage it within a limited time frame. When workers are pressured to gather particular information for the agency's records for example, they may believe that only the application of concerted prompting will achieve these purposes.

In addition, there are client-based factors that may lead to unnecessary and poorly focused questioning and probing. As an example, if a client is unwilling to volunteer information, a frequent use of prompts such as a series of questions may be a temptation although it is never a remedy. Questions and other probes can be employed to achieve particular purposes in the interview depending on its stage of development, but should not be used as a primary tool in encouraging the client's narrative or even in eliciting information.

Questions and other probes do not show empathy – that is a basic premise of this book. It is always more effective to respond consistently with warmth and understanding through reflecting (i.e. picking up on feelings and other aspects of the client's narrative) and by paraphrasing. This book focuses on the appropriate use of questions and probes in Chapter 4, because they *do* have a place in a well-managed interview, but common sense is needed in keeping their level of use limited. That said, in understanding how to use them well, it is necessary start with understanding the different types of questions and probes, where and how in the interview process they could be applied and problems with some forms of questions.

The difference between questions and probes

Questioning and probing are closely related as means of prompting the client. All questions are probes, but not all probes are questions. Egan (2007, pp. 123–124) describes four varieties of probes:

1. Statements – for example, 'I'm not sure what you mean by feeling under pressure.' Such statements are usually viewed by clients as requests for further information on the issue mentioned.
2. Requests and suggestions – for example, 'Tell me a bit more about how this pressure feels', or 'Let's discuss what's happening when you feel this way' – are more direct ways of asking for further information
3. Repeating either a word or phrase with a suitably quizzical tone – for example, 'under pressure …?' may prompt the client to elaborate on this point
4. Nonverbal prompts – for example, leaning forward and/or raising your eyebrows – may prompt the client to continue and explain things further. But whether asking questions or using probing statements, the intention is much the same – that is, *to push, poke, direct* or *entice* the client to focus on a particular issue – usually one of interest to the interviewer. This usually means the interviewer is directing the focus and not the client.

Open and closed forms of probes

Egan (2007, p. 124, 125) presents two basic guidelines about the proper use of probes in interviews – not to use too many questions or probes and if they are used to make them *open-ended*. Clearly, questions and probes have the capacity to make an interview into an inquisition, especially if they restricted, heavily directed and *closed*. Good questions/probes are usually *open* which, as the term suggests, means that they widen or open up the client's perceptions of the issues. Open questions are more likely to keep with the client's focus too – expanding on it but not changing the focus or directing it too much. What do open probes look like compared with closed ones then? The distinction between open and closed is a fairly simple one.

- An open question or probe requires some type of information as a reply.
- Closed questions are those, which can be answered with 'yes' or 'no'.

'Do you like your mother?' is a *closed* question whereas an *open* probe on this same issue would be 'How would you describe your relationship with your mother?' Often better information can be gained without probing at all, through the use of reflections and paraphrases. Closed probes are most likely to appear when the worker is fishing for different information than that which the client is freely offering. Closed questions have lead-in words that are verbs or action words – 'are', 'have', 'do' as in 'Do you work?', 'Have you tried dieting?' These verbs or *doing words* usually denote that the question is in a closed form – answerable by either Yes or No. These lead-in words, as well as other verbs like 'did', 'can', 'will', 'would', 'could' 'should', all suggest a closed probe is happening. Closed probes are also more likely to change the topic, thus suggesting they do not follow on with the client's narrative very well.

Effective, open questions usually begin with 'What' 'How' 'When' or maybe 'Who', with these words indicating an open invitation. A question like 'How's your new job going?' is open whereas 'Do you like your new job?' is closed. 'How's the exercise program going?' is open. 'Are you sticking to your exercise program?' is closed. 'Let's talk about how your study is going lately' is an open probe in a request form and 'Are you studying hard?' is a closed question. A simple open question like 'How do you feel about that?' can sometimes help the client talk about feelings, whereas a closed question such as 'Do you feel angry?' limits the focus to particular feelings only. It is interesting that typical social greetings 'How's it going?', 'How are you?' or 'What's been happening?' are all fully open questions.

Directed and restricted probes

The best sorts of probes are *fully open* leaving a wide scope for the client to talk about their feelings, issues and concerns. But, sometimes open questions and probes are used to ask for a specific piece of information. Such questions somewhat *restrict* what the client is asked to focus on, and may be used to ensure that interviewers obtain a piece of factual information. As an example, a client is asked: 'How old is your mother?', or 'How many children to you have?', or 'What suburb do you live in?' or 'What sort of benefit are you on?' These are still *open* – in that they are not able to be answered with 'yes' or 'no' – however they are heavily *restricted* or *directed* and are just minimally better than closed probes. Such probes may be useful if the interviewer *really needs a particular piece of information* – for example, to complete an agency intake form. But, to maximize the client's capacity to *volunteer free information*, both *closed* and *restricted* probes need to be kept to a minimum. In general, if probes are needed it is preferable to use fully open and unrestricted ones. But even open probes need to be used with care otherwise clients feel like they are being interrogated or as Egan says 'they feel grilled' (2007, p. 124).

Probes to avoid

Finally, there are a few types of probes that have no real place in a well-managed interview and which need to be avoided. Kadushin and Kadushin (1997, pp. 254–256) point out that misuse of questioning is common but invariably unproductive in professional interactions. Some of these appeared earlier as roadblocks, which they are, but they deserve a special mention here too. These include:

1. 'why' questions
2. leading or suggestive probes
3. advice disguised as questions
4. double and garbled questions

Why questions

'Why' questions have particular problems. Westra (1996, p. 89) suggests that 'why' questions put clients on the defensive. But 'why' questions can have other negative impacts. They ask clients to explain their own or another person's motives for doing something. As Kadushin and Kadushin (1997, p. 256) add, the 'Why questions call for greater insight than many clients possess'. These questions ask clients 'to justify thoughts, feelings, and behaviour rather than accepting that these exist' according to Westra (1996, p. 89) and may cause a client, especially one who lacks confidence, to feel under pressure to find the 'right' answers. Therefore, it would seem advisable to avoid 'why' questions at any stage, and especially in the early stages of the interview process. Consider the impact on clients of the following questions: 'Why did you get angry?', 'Why were you so late for work?' or 'Why didn't you ask her?'

Leading or suggestive probes

Kadushin and Kadushin (1997, p. 249) see the use of leading probes as a common error in interviewing. Leading questions are not actually asking the client to give their opinion or any new information, but are an attempt to have the client confirm (and conform to) the interviewer's view. In other words leading probes are a way of sliding in some instructions. The classic leading question finishes with 'isn't it?', 'doesn't it?', 'wouldn't you?' and so on. An example is 'You don't really want to put her into childcare, do you?' Leading questions confuse clients by diverting their narrative and reinforcing feelings of doubt.

Advice disguised as questions

Sometimes questions are really about advising the client *what to do*. When this is disguised as a question, the advice sounds less definite and consequently can be more insidious. For example, the interviewer says, 'Have you thought of giving up smoking?' This is a closed probe, but unpacked, it really means, 'I think you should give up smoking'. Questions as advice intrude on the client's narrative, offering no motivational encouragement.

Double and garbled questions

In double or garbled questioning, the beleaguered client is asked several questions at once. 'Do you think you manage on the money you get or do you find it a struggle?' is a typical double question. 'When you get depressed do you like going for a walk or do other exercise, or try some other activity, or does none of that work for you – or not always anyway?' This is garbled – which means it is incoherent – and probably very confusing. Double/triple/quadruple and garbled questions and other probes make it very difficult for clients to answer intelligently and undermine any clear focus for the client's reply. Many clients will still try hard to give an answer however. Others will waver until the practitioner comes back to a more reflective approach or clears up the focus by offering a more coherent question. Responses other than questions can be garbled also, such as waffly, wordy reflections or paraphrases. Garbled and incoherent responses are the product of inadequate thought before speaking. The solution is for the interviewer to slow down, take a deep breath and think carefully before speaking. This is sometimes difficult to do when interviewers feel anxious, but to get out of these muddled holes it is vital to handle own anxiety through pausing and thinking.

Accidental questions

Sometimes questions occur almost *accidentally* as a facet of intonation, as mentioned previously. The increasingly prevalent use of the 'rising inflection' turns many a perfectly good empathic reflection or paraphrase into a question and often a closed one too. It is all in the intonation of course. So that 'You feel disappointed' – a reflection of feeling – becomes 'You feel disappointed?' which now sounds like a closed question. It also makes the worker sound tentative and lacking in confidence. In attempting to show understanding and in demonstrating professionalism, responses need to be expressed in a straightforward and confident tone. To ensure that reflective responses do not sound like questions, voice tone needs to stay *even* or go *down* at the end of a response – not up.

Probes in different stages of interviewing

Egan (2007, pp. 122) describes the probe as a means of assisting clients to engage in the 'therapeutic dialogue' at different points in the professional relationship. This means knowing when and how to direct the client through the use of probes and when to respond empathically.

Purposes of questions or probes in different stages

It may be useful here to reiterate that the process of working with clients can be conceptualized as a three-stage process. These stages can be summarized as:

- Exploration of issues, establishing the professional dialogue and a 'working alliance'
- Encouraging the client to reach for self-understanding and goals
- Seeking clients' ideas about action plans to bring about solution-focused change

The worker assists movement through this process by using a range of skills, mostly reflective and empathic, as well as occasional probes to keep the client focused. In a three-stage process questions and other prompts can be seen as a way to focus the client on the different purposes of these stages. In the first exploratory stage, probes have a very different focus from goal or action focused ones.

Using probes to help clients to be more specific and detailed in exploring issues

There are several particular purposes for using probes and questions in the first stage of working with clients, all designed to focus or expand issues and open up the professional dialogue (although I continue to caution about their overuse). Apart from directing the overall interview focus, Egan (2007, pp. 125–128) suggests that in the first stage of the interview probes and questions may have the following other uses:

- To achieve behavioural concreteness: '*Describe what you do when you try to relax?*'
- To fill in missing pieces of the narrative: '*How do you feel about his reaction?*'
- To ask about client's behaviour: '*Let's talk about what you do when the family fights.*'

In the first or early stages of the process, interviewers should avoid asking a client who has just begun to talk about an issue "What have you thought of doing about it?" Here the focus is on *goals and solutions* before any relationship or trust has been established. The client may feel that the interviewer is hurrying them, is not interested in their ideas and is after quick-fix solutions.

Using probes to focus on clients' strengths, needs, wants and goals

Probing can help clients identify their strengths and their coping skills. As well, when trust is established between interviewer and client, then it may be appropriate to use a few selected probes to focus on goals and related small steps. The questions used in the following examples are probes for a goal oriented phase.

- *If you were to wake up one day and your relationship with Tom was really working well, describe two things that would be different?* This sort of 'miracle question', asking the client to imagine possibilities and to unpack the future, is described by De Jong and Berg (2008, pp. 83–85).
- *You say you want to budget better. What do you do differently when you are managing your budget well?* The probe seeks to gain a picture of the client's coping skills in this particular area of focus.
- *You have talked about wanting a 'good relationship' with your son. What would you say to him or do when he comes home from school if your relationship was good?* Here the probe is focused on a picture of actual behaviours, linked to this client's wants/desires.

But avoid probes asking the client about final solutions

De Jong and Berg (2008, p. 80) note that 'when you ask clients how they will know when their problems are solved, expect them to imagine the finish line, rather than the first sign of something different'. This indicates the importance of focusing probes on *first steps* and *early signs of success*.

- *Describe one thing you will do differently each day when your stress management plan is working.* (defining early positive behavioural signs of a plan working)
- *How will you get started on being more positive in relating to your son – let's talk about what might be a first step you could achieve today or tomorrow?* (establishing a place to start – a small first step)

This material is introductory in nature and is presented here to facilitate understanding about the different purposes of probes in reference to the different stages. A fuller explanation of how to help clients to focus on goals and action issues appears in Chapter 6.

Key points about qualities and applications of effective probes

➤ Probes are best when they are open in form and ask for free information

➤ Probes may be expressed as questions, statements and/or requests

➤ Directed and restricted probes – even if open – limit the range of information given

➤ Prompting can occur through facial expressions, raised eyebrows and minimal reflections

➤ Effective probing is intentional not accidental – so try to avoid rising voice inflections

➤ Ineffective probing may occur when workers are anxious, take insufficient time to think before speaking, feel pressured to make things happen and have low tolerance of silence

➤ Double, garbled, leading, advice framed and 'why' questions are best avoided

➤ Probes are used most effectively to direct and focus the interview

➤ Probing has different uses and applications in the three stages of interviewing

---

Recording processes in the interview

Sometime social workers and others need to record some of the detail from interviews with clients and this entails careful management of a process that can concern clients.

Related to the desire to ask too many questions is the perceived pressure to remember what is said in an interview and this often raises questions about how material can best be recorded. Students frequently ask me: 'Should I take notes during an interview?' or 'How can I remember everything the client tells me unless I take notes?' But note taking is hard to do well once the practitioner is involved fully in responding empathically to the client. This may mean it is necessary to interrupt the interview's flow to take detailed notes, negatively impacting on both empathy and on the general flow. Students seem to fear they will not remember enough to be able to summarize when required, but a well-structured interaction based on some good planning should provide a sort of template that acts as a memory jog for the practitioner to make notes following its conclusion. The worker can refer to the list of topics and the breakdown into sub-areas, which may have been discussed during the interview, as a guide. If the interaction must be taped or video recorded, express client permission or consent is required. Whatever sort of recording is used, collaborative, transparent processes which include the client in decisions are needed. This applies to the use of planning notes, other note taking and audio/video recording in ongoing cases with clients in agency settings in both single session interviews and in a series.

Pressure of notetaking

Stewart and Cash (2003, pp. 118–119) in discussing note taking in interviews suggest this activity may have advantages but generally involves considerable stress for the interviewer in trying to get everything down accurately without losing focus on the client. In professional practice, there may be a requirement to take notes for agency, practitioner records or for research purposes. In general, written notes are best made *directly following* the interview, unless they are simple tick box responses. Okun and Kantrowitz (2008, pp. 90 and 91) discuss some of the features of recording notes from interviews and also note that the 'purpose of record keeping is to provide documentation of a helpee's progress and to provide continuity of treatment' (p. 295).

If the interviewer does need to take notes, proper consideration of the client's concerns for confidentiality must be featured. For the interviewer to be able to assure clients of this confidentiality in relation to certain issues, any recording material needs to be managed ethically and respectfully. It is not uncommon for there to be agency requirements where the worker is expected to record certain details for official or working files. Some agencies have a pro forma (either on paper or computer), which is used to record client details.

Depending on state and federal jurisdictions, notes taken during or following an interview may be called for in the future in reference to due legal process, especially if there is worker compensation or another legal case pending. This means being very mindful about recording details on issues where the client does not want these disclosed either in a court of law or in other similar forums dealing with issues such as mediation, arbitration, family court matters or financial settlements. It underlines the importance of showing the client what is being recorded as is suggested by Stewart and Cash (2003, p. 118). The interviewer needs to inform clients of any requirements to record matters and to show them the information that is being recorded for the official agency records, as well as any other notes recorded for the worker's own purposes. Clients should be informed who else will have access to the notes. At the end of the interview, clients can be asked to sign that they confirm that the notes are accurate and do not contain anything they object to and that they give their consent for specified persons to have access to the notes.

Taping or video recording interviews

In some settings, all interviews are recorded on audio or video tape as a matter of course as this ensures a record is kept but absolves the interviewer from feeling responsible for its accuracy. Stewart and Cash (2003, p. 119) also recommend the use of audio taping instead of note-taking as they see this as preserving the accuracy of the client's material without undermining the interviewer's attention. Of course, they mention that the client's permission must be gained and this needs to include a full explanation of how and where the taped record will be transcribed and stored and who will have access to it. Clients should be asked to sign a consent form about recording the interview and who may view/hear it. Ivey and Ivey (2008, p. 125) suggest that in counselling work some clients may find value in taking a copy of the recording home to view/listen to it, as this has potential for 'enhancing learning from the interview'.

General consideration of all types of recording in interviewing

In general, the primary purposes of note taking or tape recording in interviews are three-fold:

■ to provide documentation of both the client's initial situation and of progress made during the first and in subsequent interviews;
■ to assist in providing continuity of management in situations where staff members are moved around or where clients do not always see the same worker;
■ to provide an official record able to be used, with the client's consent, in case conferences or where there are legal and other concerns about assessment, decision making and any actions that flow from these.

Key points about recording interviews

➤ Always record the date, time and duration of interviews, the client's name, age, address and any other demographic details as required by the agency

➤ The purpose of the interview should be recorded as well as outcomes of the session including some key client information and decisions

➤ Any client information recorded should be objective and behavioural

➤ Avoid recording value judgements or interpretations

➤ Observe sensitivity to ethical and legal issues and the risks to the client

➤ Show the client all recorded notes and completed pro formas at the end of the interview

➤ Ask the client to sign to show agreement about accuracy and content of notes as well as names/positions of all those with access to these

➤ If the interview is video or audio recorded, gain client consent for the process

CHAPTER OVERVIEW

Lack of confidence may lead interviewers to ask too many questions, and in particular too many closed ones. Responding to clients' feelings in a simple reflection is a much better first effort when the interviewer is lost for words and/or feels under pressure in an interview situation. This chapter has described how questions and other probes *can be* employed for useful purposes as well as to make transitions to new areas of focus. It has been stressed that most clients will narrate more freely if they are offered non-judgemental, accepting, warm and insightful responses from an interviewer demonstrating interest in them and their issues. This chapter has emphasized that in beginning the interview, but at other points also, attentive listening and observing and the use of a range of reflective responses remains the *foundation* of professional competence in interviewing.

This book now moves on to examine the key processes involved in managing the direction of the interview especially in reference to a *single* episode. This is not about putting aside the emphasis on empathic responding. Rather it is about holding all these processes in mind and adding the set of tasks related to employing probes and other response types to direct and focus an interview so as to achieve its purposes.

CHAPTER 5

Managing the Focus of the Interview

This chapter examines some of the key processes involved in managing the focus of a single interview effectively. A well-managed interview requires structure and clear working goals to remain focused, especially when it has particular purposes. In my experience, this is a neglected aspect, on which many other texts on interviewing provide little guidance. Many seem to imply that if an interviewer has effective skills in reflecting and paraphrasing then this will carry the day. The empathic skills discussed so far, although essential in many respects, may not be sufficient to ensure that the interview is directed well. Required also are a set of processes that direct the interview to attain its desired outcomes. These skills of directing and focusing are incorporated into an approach which emphasizes empathic work but values the interviewer's ability to collaborate with clients about the goals of the interview and to achieve these.

The importance of a preliminary mapping of the issues

Broad issues need to be identified in advance of the actual interview and then broken down into smaller ones for discussion. The use of an interview plan, where possible designed in advance or as part of a collaborative effort between client and interviewer, facilitates efficient use of the time available and supports the strength of the working alliance. As big issues contain a wide range of possible points for discussion in an interview, it is often necessary to break these down into a logical and thoughtful sequence of smaller issues or into a kind of *mind map*. For example, if the area of health is in focus, then it could be broken down into the following list of smaller points, although this is just a set of possibilities.

When the background of a client is known, the list may be more selectively customized for particular purposes.

- overall health estimation on a scale of 1–10
- current health/medical problems – if any – and current medical treatment
- medication prescribed and being used
- first small steps in managing existing health problems
- reliance on alcohol or use of other recreational drugs
- impact of alcohol or drug use on aspects of health and fitness
- first steps in managing drug and alcohol use
- levels and sources of current stress
- impact of stress on physical and psychological health
- first steps in managing stress
- dominant moods and feelings over an average week
- strategies and steps in managing moods and feelings

The worker could generate this list on a whiteboard or on a piece of paper able to be shown to the client but not necessarily visible to the client at all times, as this may encourage a less spontaneous narrative. It may be turned around to share with the client and to guide discussion at different points of focus throughout the interview.

Clients may be asked to choose where to start, but the interviewer needs to be prepared to suggest a starting point if they cannot or may not decide. This might be quite general as in: *How about telling me about how the last week has been for you.* If there is no choice available to the client on this starting point, or when time is short and certain issues must be discussed, then the practitioner will need to suggest the first issue fairly firmly as in: *First up, tell me about your family situation.* If there is some sense of follow through from a previous interaction it might be more like: *Let's pick up on the issue of diet and fitness we were discussing last week. How has the diet gone for you this week?*

The interviewer needs to avoid following a plan slavishly and instead be prepared to adapt it if the client seems better served by a different order or focus of issues. The use of a structured plan implies some application of probes but it is important to surround these with reflections or paraphrases. In other words, a series of questions in a kind of 'question–answer' format is to be avoided. Finally, the interviewer should not see a planned series of issues as something to run through, like a kind of shopping list. Instead it is referred to as a guide to each area as selected by the client when the process is a collaborative one.

Of course, when clients just walk in the door with little advance notice, then planning may be minimal although never totally neglected. All clients deserve to be asked what they hope to gain from the interview. Even when clients arrive without notice, agreeing with them on the scope of the interview makes it more likely that they will cooperate in achieving its purposes.

Defining focus points in the interview

In conducting a good interview, basic verbal skills such as reflections and paraphrases are deliberately and purposefully applied to bring about certain conditions and events. As well, a number of additional processes to structure the interaction are required in every interview, whatever its purpose. These include starting the interview well, keeping it flowing over the number of relevant points of focus and firmly and courteously concluding it.

In more detail, the steps and processes in an interview include:

1. Initiating the interaction effectively (meet, greet, seat), collaborating with the client on the purpose and scope of the interview and dealing with consent and confidentiality
2. Focusing on relevant issues with strategic use of probes whilst maintaining an empathic platform of responding
3. Smoothly managing transitions between points in the interview
4. Bringing the interaction to a close, summarizing the interview, affirming the client for work done and ending up courteously.

Initiating the interaction effectively

The beginning phase of an interview colours the whole relationship between practitioner and client and to some extent ensures it begins and progresses well. Some of these processes have been discussed briefly in Chapter 1.

Getting started

There are a range of issues to consider when initiating a professional conversation. The management of the physical setting has been discussed previously, as has the interviewer's attending, observing and listening. This is all about beginning the encounter with courtesy and respect. Practitioners in some settings will not always have total control over all aspects of the physical environment, but where it is possible the situation needs to be free from external noises and other distractions such as office phones and mobiles. The best spaces for work have a comfortable temperature, are clean and are appropriately furnished with chairs of a correct size and shape and have a whiteboard or paper on which to write points and ideas.

It is important not to presume to know how clients may wish to be addressed. For instance, a 70-year-old client named Mrs Delia Brown *may* wish to be called Mrs Brown but she *may* prefer to be addressed as Delia. Interviewers need to avoid using diminutives of clients' names unless they request this. For example, a woman named Jennifer may hate to be called Jenny but may also prefer it, so it is important to ask about preferred names. Likewise, the client needs to know how the interviewer wishes to be addressed. If the interviewer prefers to be called by their first name, it may be that clients from some cultural groups may feel very awkward doing so. In such cases, the interviewer should accept the formal term at least initially and avoid pushing the issue as this may only exacerbate the client's discomfort on this matter. In time, if client and worker get to know each other better, increased familiarity may bring about change in how each is addressed.

Defining purpose and scope

A vital aspect in ensuring a useful focus entails inviting the client to discuss what they hope to achieve in this interview. This is applicable to most interviews except a research-focused one where sometimes the topics and issues are pre-determined. This invitation to discuss purposes and outcomes relates strongly to the interviewer seeing clients as experts in their own lives as discussed in De Jong and Berg (2008, pp. 18–19). To begin this process, the interviewer introduces the idea that the interview has a purpose and so will be kept to mutually agreed areas of focus as much as possible. The client is asked to describe what they hope to achieve from this interview if it goes well for them and from any further work with the interviewer. This reinforces the idea that the interview is goal focused and that there can be achievable outcomes from it, with relevance to the client and their issues. This opening question might be worded: 'If this interview goes well for you what do you hope you will gain from it?' For the sake of transparency, interviewers can also share whether they hope to achieve something from it too. When the client is known to the worker, there may be a known list of issues needing to be explored and agreement on which ones need to be focused on first. If the interviewer has designed the interview plan in advance of the interview, it needs to be reviewed when the client arrives, by checking that the plan will support the attainment of the client's goals.

Planning the interpreted interview

When it becomes necessary to work with an interpreter, there may be added pressure on the practitioner to promote clear direction and this is based on good background planning. The interpreted interview needs to be planned to allow time for the interpreting process to take place – *about double* the usual interview time. Clients may struggle to work with interpreters because of uncomfortable experiences in the past and lack of confidence in the confidentiality aspects. If possible, deal with any issues requiring some discussion with the interpreter before clients arrive to avoid having conversations they cannot understand (or may partially understand) in front of them. Practitioner and interpreter should not be found sitting in the interview room when the client arrives, as this may damage client confidence in the neutrality of both interviewer and interpreter.

When all parties are present, simple introductions are completed and everyone is asked to take a seat. In general, the practitioner sits facing the client, with the interpreter the same distance away from both the client and the interviewer so all three people form a sort of triangle. Once seated, it is appropriate to introduce the interpreter and, through the interpreter, to explains his or her role to the client, allowing time and space for any questions. As well, at the beginning of the interview, the worker explains her role to the client so it is clear who will be managing the interview. The interviewer speaks almost exclusively to the client, *not* to the interpreter and maintains eye gaze (where culturally appropriate) with the client but not with the interpreter. If there needs to be a conversation between worker and interpreter then this is explained to the client first, with apologies for interrupting the interview process.

The interaction begins by asking the client, with the interpreter translating, what will need to be achieved in the interview for the client to consider it a worthwhile and successful activity. Early in the interview, check with both the client and the interpreter whether the pace is appropriate, stressing that the client can ask for any clarification about roles or processes if this is required at any point. If there is a need to question the client or interviewer on any issue, the interviewer should ensure clear and simple probes and other plain language at all times. Jargon and complicated language are avoided at all times.

In all interactions, beginning processes are vital to the development of the professional relationship and may influence the success of the whole interview. Clarity, courtesy and respect at this stage especially, demonstrate professional integrity to clients.

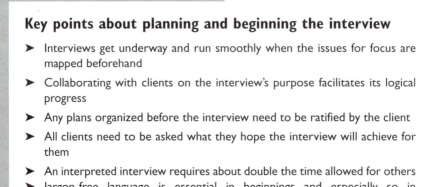

Key points about planning and beginning the interview

➤ Interviews get underway and run smoothly when the issues for focus are mapped beforehand

➤ Collaborating with clients on the interview's purpose facilitates its logical progress

➤ Any plans organized before the interview need to be ratified by the client

➤ All clients need to be asked what they hope the interview will achieve for them

➤ An interpreted interview requires about double the time allowed for others

➤ Jargon-free language is essential in beginnings and especially so in interpreted interactions

➤ Aspects of structure and courteous introductions are essential in all interactions

Tensions between empathy and direction

A well-planned and competently managed interview benefits both client and worker in that it assists clients to explore issues more fully and supports the worker in moving efficiently over issues within the allotted time frame. This is especially so when interview sessions are brief in some work settings. A set of points, each with some sub-issues, provides a view of the scope of an interview. This plan allows the interviewer to focus on the liberal use of empathic skills without fearing the non-achievement of the aims of the interview.

Once underway, the task becomes one of remaining empathic whilst also maintaining some control over the interview's flow and purpose. I realize this sounds like a contradiction, but it is one of the tensions implicit in being an effective interviewer. Generally speaking, exploring very few issues substantially in an interview is more worthwhile than skimming over an inventory of many. The intention, in a well-managed interview, is to remain within the client's frame even though there are some requirements for structure to attain these aims. Conveying understanding and positive acceptance of clients' ideas, opinions and feelings through the use of empathic skills remains the central concern. Balanced against this empathic project is the need to keep the interview focused in useful directions, through the use of an interview plan that is also firmly progressed. Knowing how to manage transitions between topics and sub–topics requires an essential set of skills. The next section focuses on the range of processes and skills involved in managing this movement or *transition* between points of the interview plan.

The tension between staying with the client and applying direction comes from the dual pressure to make a good connection and deal with the client empathically but also to gather particular information required by the agency for example. So being asked to focus on self and to talk about feelings and experiences may cause many clients to experience difficulty, despite all the modern pressures to focus on self that I have discussed previously in this book. Many clients feel fearful and anxious about the threat of disorganization in discussing things long buried and are tentative about unearthing such issues. They may also fear being rejected by their family members, work mates and other people, for needing to seek outside help in managing their lives. Clients may also fear change – as do most of us. Especially when clients have low self–esteem, they feel there is much to lose in facing change and about exposing their thoughts and feelings to another person. It feels very unsafe. Clients need early signs that it is all going to be worth the effort and that the interview process is safe. This takes us back to the need for practitioner skills in empathy and acceptance and establishing a genuinely positive framework. Also, a client who is cooperative for most of the interview sometimes becomes emotionally caught up in a particular issue. This may mean they either talk to excess or clam up and both verbose and very quiet clients can be equally difficult to manage. When clients are largely silent or unresponsive, this can place pressure on practitioners especially if there is organizational pressure to work inside a time frame. Whether this is a constant feature or just a temporary aberration in an interview, the phenomenon of clients who seem unresponsive and those who are very talkative both need to be competently and courteously managed.

Interviewing clients who seem unresponsive

The ability of interviewers to avoid heavy prompting and to remain responsive is seriously tested when clients are hard to get talking. Getting and/or keeping the process moving with a very quiet client can feel a bit like pulling teeth! Corey and Corey (1999, p. 103) agree with me on this and suggest such clients can make workers feel very anxious and strongly responsible for getting the client to open up. In watching many examples of students working with non-responsive clients, I have witnessed the struggle they encounter in trying to get quiet clients to open up a bit and the mistakes made in attempting to do so. They ask too many questions generally and often slide into a run of closed questions – 'Do you like any sport?' 'Have you seen any good movies lately?' and so on. Corey and Corey (1999, p. 104) agree that very quiet and unresponsive clients may lead workers to overuse questions and neglect responsive listening. Probing usually pushes quiet clients further into a passive position. The tendency to ask a series of questions is best avoided then, as the interview will quickly become a question-focused routine, with the interviewer in the driver's seat going nowhere! Patient, empathic work may in time entice the quiet client to open up.

Corey and Corey (1999, p. 103) suggest a range of reasons for clients being quiet – from fear of worker judgement, waiting for workers to tell them what to do, rehearsing in their heads what to say, or just lack of practice in talking about self. Sometimes a remedy is available in the consistent use of silence with occasional feeling and content reflections or paraphrasing (whenever enough material can be gathered to do so). Very quiet clients, with low levels of trust in the worker as well as in the process and/or the agency, who also feel coerced to attend, may take several interviews to open up. This may be so even if the interviewer does everything possible to encourage them. I also believe there is an age and gender variable here. Young people – especially adolescents and young males – seem to struggle most with self-expressiveness in the interviewing situation. This is especially so if they feel at all coerced (by parents or teachers) to attend the interview session and it is a struggle to find ways to make the process worth their while. Taking the adolescent client out for a walk or for a coffee break may ease tension and open up the communication lines.

Clients from minority cultures may take longer to trust the worker and to open up (Corey and Corey 1999, p. 188). Even in cases where workers themselves are from a minority culture, a cultural background at variance with the mainstream may cause clients to approach the agency and the interview with caution. Trust is earned through the interviewer demonstrating skill and competence in empathic responding and in positive, goal-focused processes in counselling. Of course some clients from different ethnic groups may also have language difficulties requiring the assistance of an interpreter to be successfully interviewed and this entails special consideration.

The issue of client 'resistance'

Quiet or unresponsive clients are sometimes perceived as being resistant. De Jong and Berg (2008, p. 72) discuss the importance of not labelling clients as 'resistant'. Client unresponsiveness, or apparent non-compliance with the expectations of the interview setting and/or the interviewer, is more likely to be a product of the relationship between the client and the worker, rather than a client characteristic per se. This is especially so when coercion by government or agency rules pushes the client to attend an interview. As De Jong and Berg (2008, p. 73) note, 'Impasses and apparent failures in our work do not result from client resistance to our best professional efforts to make them well. Rather, they result from our failure to listen to clients and take seriously what they tell us'.

Many texts mention client resistance and reluctance as though these came with the client and were a sign of their inability to accept the need to change. Egan (2007, p. 190) refers to reluctance and resistance as 'pervasive phenomena' that are almost inevitably part of any helping interaction. Okun and Kantrowitz (2008, p. 95) suggest too that resistance 'can occur initially … or at any time in the helping relationship, and can vary in intensity and duration'. The phenomenon may be part of a client's pattern rather than inherent in the interviewing relationship as such, but may also develop as a result of non-empathic and otherwise inappropriate or incompetent responses from the practitioner. De Jong and Berg (2008, p. 72) also assert that the concept of client resistance may be a self-serving one in that if the client improves then the interviewer can claim the credit but if there is no improvement then the client is deemed to be resistant or at best reluctant. Instead De Jong and Berg suggest that workers need to explore their own inability to connect with their clients and to quieten 'our own frames of reference, so that we listen with solution-building ears and invite clients to participate in solution-building conversations' (De Jong and Berg 2008, p. 73). Unresponsive, quiet and so-called reticent clients pose challenges for inexperienced interviewers and more seasoned ones alike, although the very talkative client also tests the interviewer's ability to balance empathy and direction.

Focusing the over-talkative client

I have also seen many examples of interviewing work where the worker becomes speechless and ineffective with clients who talk incessantly. In severe cases, the interviewer cannot seem to get a word (or a good response) into the discussion and thus cannot influence its focus or direction. Unless the interviewer keeps actively involved in the client's narrative of their experiences, there is the risk that a professional focus and any control of the interview will be lost. Corey and Corey (1999, p. 105) suggest that very talkative clients may lead the worker to a pretence of listening and I have seen this too – with the interviewer operating only as a sort of nodding puppet. Many talk a lot because they feel anxious, have little experience of being listened to and lack socialization skills regarding how to have a mutual conversation. So part of managing clients who are talkative, at least to start with, may include educating them about turn taking and the place of thinking and listening in conversation.

Sometimes it is necessary to use a courteous but firm interruption, followed quickly with an invitation to share on a different topic – thus suggesting structure and establishing a pattern of interaction. Sometimes it is necessary to stop the interview and to explain that a regular paraphrase or summary is necessary if the interviewer is to be useful to them. Some clients have current or past issues which are very emotionally charged and which they have trouble *not* talking about. If this is the case, the interviewer listens respectfully, taking care to interject at least some reflective responses over a reasonable period of time, thus demonstrating acceptance of their interest. After a decent space of time, an attempt is then made to move on to a different topic. This may be done successfully by summarizing briefly and swiftly moving to another relevant area by using an open probe. Some talkative clients are lonely and just need space to talk if the situation and time allow it. With space to talk and some gentle education about the worker's role, these clients may be able to focus productively on a relevant range of issues. When time is tight however, the talkative client may need to be managed more firmly, although always courteously.

Key points about balancing focus and empathy

➤ Tension often exists between moving the interview along and responding empathically

➤ Tension between empathy and directional focus may derive from agency pressures including time restraints as well as some client variables

➤ Client variables such as quietness or apparent unresponsiveness and over-talkativeness require gentle management with a continuing focus on empathy

➤ Quiet clients rarely respond to inquisitional questioning

➤ Quiet clients are sometimes viewed as resistant but resistance is more a feature of poor interview management and interviewer attitudes

➤ Very talkative clients need courteous management but sometimes firm direction

➤ It may be necessary to courteously interrupt talkative clients in order to respond and maintain direction

Managing transitions between points in the interview

A central process in managing the tension between direction and empathy is how well the shifts in focus are facilitated. A transition is the point where a shift of focus is made, using processes to gently guide the client. In their own right, transition points can be difficult moments to manage and for some practitioners it may feel wrong to direct the interview firmly. Kadushin and Kadushin (1997, p. 158) suggest that many practitioners maintain that 'the need for focus that is served by using transitions may be antithetical to the need for rapport' and that at times they believe 'the interviewer may have to sacrifice focus for rapport'. I agree that each topic shift and transition is potentially disruptive and unsettling to the client and may make the client feel less free. Nonetheless, focus is essential to the achievement of interview goals and purposes and managed with courtesy and care it need not disrupt the client's equilibrium too much. However because a shift in focus can be a bit disturbing, all transitions should have a clear aim in terms of a coherent interview plan and should not be used unnecessarily. Nor should a change of focus occur when there is insufficient time available to explore anything new.

The nature of transitions

It is important to think about 'transitions' as a more formalized and deliberately professional use of what the layperson calls 'changing the subject' and in this sense it is also related to 'interrupting' to some extent. Clearly, nobody likes being interrupted, though it happens frequently in ordinary conversation. In the professional interview, it is essential to avoid interrupting for any purpose not essential for the interview's success and it needs to be done with courtesy and respect.

This client has been discussing her family and financial situation and has started to go round in circles a bit – and the practitioner makes a decision to wind it up and move her along

> **Client**: It's been a big struggle financially – for me and the twins – and I've been feeling a bit desperate about it all – mainly because I can't see it getting any easier. My part-time job helps a bit as I said but overall it's hard to manage. You see – I got divorced three years ago – I know I haven't talked much about him yet. He's supposed to give me a regular amount. He occasionally throws a few dollars our way, but it's not regular like. Mostly I have to manage on my own. The girls have just started high school this year and there are lots of extra expenses. They want extra things too, and I really can't afford them. They don't understand – being teenagers and they get angry with me – [tearfully] it's not fair!! When they were smaller it was easier. [Client looks upset and blows her nose.] It's the teenage years – they are harder to please now, and it's more difficult financially these days too. Their father doesn't help at all really. He's a gambler you see and a drinker and never has much to spare either, except for when he has a win – and then he's Mister Generous – with the kids anyway! And that makes it harder for me to keep us to a tight budget, as he confuses the situation for them. I get so angry with him sometimes. He knows how I feel, but he's weak – just weak!

The practitioner, attempting to shift the focus off complaining and onto more productive issues makes the following reply: 'And that makes you angry – on top of all the financial pressures – OK. I might try to summarize here. You're divorced and have a family (your two girls), you have a part-time job but you don't get much help from your ex, and money is a constant issue now the girls are in high school. It's fairly tight overall, but I would bet you have some good skills in managing it all. What's one thing you do to cope with the financial pressure?'

The transition is made here by summarizing and then mentioning the issue for focus before using an open probe to encourage the client onto it. Kadushin and Kadushin (1997) is one of the few texts that focus quite specifically on managing transitions between issues in an interview. The authors take a rather 'problem-solving' approach overall compared with mine and with those expressed in Ivey and Ivey (2003) and De Jong and Berg (2008). However, the transition processes described by Kadushin and Kadushin (1997, pp. 152–163) can be adapted to a more positive solution-focused approach. If transitions are not managed by the interviewer, the client (and the interviewer) may inappropriately move from topic to topic, wander into unrelated areas, or get stuck on an issue. This is most likely when the helper is inactive or passive, especially if this is coupled with a verbose client. Brief, frequent empathic responses, along with well–timed summaries that lead smoothly into transitions to the next related area, are the hallmarks of a well-managed interview.

Types of transitions

Kadushin and Kadushin (1997, p. 154) suggest that transitions 'refer not only to a change in topic but also to a change in affect level within a topic'. By this they mean the interviewer may shift the focus onto feelings especially if these seem not to be part of the client's narrative. This can easily occur through the use of targeted paraphrases or summaries as part of a normal transition. Here a health counsellor is talking with a nurse and moves the focus to feelings. *'Thanks for telling me about your work – it seems to be very busy and keeps you on your toes. Let's talk about how you feel at the end of the work day – what would be your most usual emotion, say at the end of a shift as you walk out the hospital door?'*

Kadushin and Kadushin (1997, pp. 154–161) also discuss a range of transition types and for the sake of clarity, three forms mentioned by Kadushin and Kadushin are summarized here:

Smooth: This is where the transition flows smoothly from the present issue to a related one and is appropriately timed and managed in the interview.

The client is talking to a social worker about her daily pattern of life: '*So because I haven't been working for the last three months, these sloppy things have crept into my life. I really think sometimes that I have become addicted to daytime television. As well I think I've wrecked my sleep patterns – by staying up after midnight and then getting up late – lost the old work ethic! I don't like all the weight I've gained – all those TV snacks, drinks and things'.*

The social worker responds with the intention of moving the focus more clearly onto health matters. *'You feel concerned because your life now lacks direction. Let's focus on your health in a bit more detail. On a scale of 1–10 with 1 being the worst – how would you currently rate your general health?'*

Abrupt: This type of transition is a sudden change of topic. It may be a dramatic shift that does not logically follow. In the instance above here, an abrupt shift would be a response like: *'What's your financial situation like?'* Sometimes abrupt shifts in the topic are appropriately related to the previous one in some way but the process of shifting to the new topic offers no warning to the client that the shift is about to occur. It may also lack any verbal bridges – such as in a warning or paraphrasing what has been discussed so far – before moving onto the new area. With reference to the previous client example, an abrupt although better linked response might be: *'How much do you drink each day?'* Abrupt shifts of focus like this should be avoided through the use of more appropriate links – such as empathic summaries and signals of intention to transition between issues.

Reversional: This is a transition that moves the client back to a previous topic, perhaps because it was not fully explored, or because the client moved on to a new area and the worker considers this was premature. *'Thanks for telling me about your sister and her current troubles. I can see you care a lot for her. I'd like go back a bit here – to your health issues and to what you see as your best health feature.'* A reversional transition may be either smooth or abrupt in terms of its connection to other issues or in the interviewer's transition processes.

Steps and processes in the well-managed transition

The set of processes involved in managing a transition are as follows:

- Mentally select the new area for focus
- Summarize or paraphrase the previous issue
- Signal that a change of topic is to occur
- Make an open probe to the new area
- Paraphrase the client's narrative on the new area

Selecting the issue for focus

A logical interview plan supports the smooth movement over issues during the interview. The interviewer begins the process of transition by watching for a logical point to begin, such as the client slowing down, the client pausing, or after a fairly long passage of narrative on a particular issue that seems finished.

Clients sometimes select their own point of transition – often quite abruptly – by shifting the interview to another topic. Kadushin and Kadushin (1997, pp. 160–163) refer to these as 'Interviewee-Initiated Transitions'. They suggest clients may make these shifts because they are bored, need a break from serious things and want to talk about something lighter or more pleasant. They may also wish to avoid an emotionally hard issue or have something else they want to talk about, although this is far less likely if there has been collaborative planning about the focus. Generally, if this client-initiated shift fits the overall plan for the interview, or seems to be a logical shift, the interviewer may go along with it. The interviewer may wish to acknowledge the shift and influence how it goes however, by saying something like: *'I see we have shifted the topic somewhat – onto work hassles. Let's stay with it for now but we will go back later to talk about your alcohol use.'* The practitioner may also wish to take the client back to a previous issue if they have moved off this issue prematurely or if the current one seems irrelevant. After the point is selected, the next transition step is that of summarizing the client's narrative on the current theme before moving away from it.

Summarizing the main points from an issue or aspect of the client's story

Usually, the step of summarizing the key points focuses on the current issue being discussed or several issues if it is towards the end of the interview. The summary often starts with a phrase such as: *'OK, let me see if I have got most things straight. You've described the stresses for you in having your mother move in and managing her ill-health and you have talked about the mixture of feelings there for you ... your frustration, love, guilt and anxiety and you have begun to identify some ways to help both you and her to better handle the situation'*. A good summary is not just a shopping list of things talked about, but should selectively focus on some key feelings and achievements if these have been identified. Interim summaries grasp key aspects of feelings, situations and behaviours in the client's story so far. Sometimes a good summary sets some clients off again on their narrative, especially if they have been a bit fixated on some things. This may mean the interviewer loses the transition 'moment' as it were. If so, it may be advisable to avoid emphasizing feelings in the next summary attempt by making a very brief summary or even trying the shift without a summary especially if the helper is struggling to regain control of the interview.

Signalling the worker's intention to shift the focus

Usually, following the summary, the interviewer signals that a change of focus is imminent. Nonverbal movement may help to indicate the interviewer's intention to make a transition. A verbal phrase is more usually employed to signal the interviewer's intention to change the focus, such as something like: *'I think it's time to move onto another area'*, or *'Let's move onto something else now'*.

If necessary, something stronger may be needed to halt the flow of the client's narrative, especially when they seem stuck. This should still be done politely and gently. This is where the interviewer may combine a minimal sort of summary and the signal to shift with something like this: *'Thanks Tom – that's really clear – I feel like I've got a good understanding of what's happening in your work and I think we could move on now to another area. Tell me about what you do to manage your tension and stress'.* In this case, the interviewer does not summarize or paraphrase – just mentions the current focus – before trying to shift the interview along. This may be a deliberate approach at times where the practitioner sees that a more empathic response may inspire a verbose client to continue sharing in even greater detail.

Sometimes it may be necessary to interrupt quite firmly to regain some control over the direction of the interview. Kadushin and Kadushin (1997, p. 156) refer to this as a 'transitional interruption'. They suggest this approach should be used with caution, perhaps in dealing with a garrulous client who 'talks and talks about things that are of little consequence to the objectives of the interview'. In such a situation, the interviewer uses a lead-in statement like: *'I want to ask you to stop there'* or *'I need to interrupt you there'*. A gesture such as holding up a hand – in a sort of stop position – may be necessary to stem the flow in some instances. The collaborative interview plan can be called on here to add authority to a suggested topic shift. *'We agreed to discuss your health issues today and so far we have not focused on these yet'*. Then the interviewer moves onto something like: *'I want you to tell me about ...'* or a statement similar to those mentioned in the next step, which is about probing to shift to a new issue.

Using an open probe to make the shift

An open probe is the final step in shifting the focus. This might be something like *'Tell me about your budgeting skills'*. *'How do you manage stress in your life?'* or *'Tell me about your relationship with your son'*. Note these are open probes – in either question or request form – and act to *briefly* and *clearly* signal the next topic for focus. Garbled or double questions are avoided here as these may confuse the client anyway at a point of some psychological disarray brought about by the transition process, especially if it has dragged them away from an issue in which they were engrossed.

In this following example, the interviewer has decided that it is time to shift the focus from work to health-related issues. So she begins by saying: *'OK – you have explained really well how you feel resentful because they have treated you discourteously at work but that you also feel pretty powerful because you have dealt with the situation assertively and have used positive self-talk to keep your spirits up'* (summary of feelings, situation and behaviour with strengths focus). *'I'd like to move to some health issues'* (signal). *'Let's talk about how these issues at work might be affecting your general health and well-being'* (clear open probe with a connection from previous area to ease the shift).

Empathic responding to the client's follow-on material

Following the shift to this new area, it is essential that the interviewer listens carefully to what the client says and uses empathic reflections or paraphrases that demonstrate understanding of the client's narrative. It is vital to avoid any further questioning at this point, as the client usually feels rather 'pushed around' by the transition process and now needs the chance to talk without being prompted – or poked – any further. If the client does not seem able to talk about the new issue, the interviewer should resist the urge to move to another area and instead consider how best to deal with this slow or dead spot. The interviewer could just stay silent and practice patience. If the client does not say anything after this small pause, a simple feeling reflection can be offered if there are some nonverbal indications to base this on.

Good attending and patience is needed for moments when the interview seems to slow down. The nervous client (and helper) may react anxiously when nothing is said for a short while, in which case reassurance is needed that silence and thoughtful moments are good processes in the interview. It might also be appropriate sometimes to draw the client back to a previous issue by summarizing what has been said most recently. Once the client is talking again, *only* empathic responses are used to explore each issue fairly substantially before any further attempts to move the focus.

Key points about managing the interview's focus

➤ Transition management processes are vital in directing the interview focus

➤ Transition steps are: *Summary; Signal* (the intention to shift the focus); *Shift* (by using an open probe) and *Paraphrase* (to help client follow on with the narrative)

➤ Transitions can be smooth, abrupt or reversional – but the best are smooth and logical

➤ The transition process needs to be clear and gentle to avoid pushing the client around

➤ Once a shift has been made, it is essential to follow on with empathic responding

---

Concluding the interview

The final point of transition is to conclude or end the interview. It is very important to manage this well, in that it may determine how the client feels following the interview and their commitment to attend another session if this is required. It is important that the practitioner notes when it is near the time for the interview to finish and that both helper and client are psychologically prepared to finish the interaction. Preparing to finish may entail warning clients at about five minutes before the end of the interview that the end is approaching. Very chatty clients might need additional encouragement or several attempts to get them to wind down. The signal about this ending phase may begin with a time warning, such as *'We've got about five minutes left'*, or *'We need to be finishing up soon'.*

As the end of the interview approaches, the helper needs to prepare mentally for delivering a final summary of the client's achievements in the interview. This may require a quick reference to the written plan as a memory jog. Before delivering the summary, it is advisable to warn the client that a final summary is being attempted (that is to conclude the interview), otherwise the client may launch into a further narrative, encouraged by an empathic and strength-focused summary. If this occurs, a second summary attempt will be needed when the client finishes. Respect and good humour are sometimes needed to manage this situation when it occurs.

As in other interviews, when using an interpreter the worker also affirms the client for goal achievements in the interview and relates this to their strengths and the skills demonstrated in their narrative of life circumstances. A summary of the interview is made by the helper and through the interpreter. At the end of the interview, the client is asked how satisfied they are with the interview outcomes and what other issues they need to follow up through further interviews. Finally, all stand up while farewells are made. If there are any further issues to discuss with the interpreter, some agreement about how to catch up about these is made before the interview if possible, to allow the interview to conclude and for the client and interpreter to depart together.

In much human service work in the field, social workers and others may have in mind something the client needs to talk about in a subsequent interview and this may be mentioned before the interview's conclusion. As well, at this point the client may be asked to complete some homework activity for discussion in the next session. In concluding, the client is wished well and if appropriate is guided out of the room as farewells are expressed. Clients managed with courtesy and care throughout the interaction and in this final passage of it, leave the encounter feeling positive and with an increase in self-esteem. For this to occur, the worker will have responded empathically in the interview, reinforcing positive things throughout and affirming the client genuinely and appropriately.

Finally, to conclude this chapter which has exposed even further expectations of interviewing competence in the human services, it is important to revisit the pressures most practitioners feel at some point. Pressure is implicit in managing the interview focus as well as maintaining an empathic style of responding – and keeping all these balls in the air can cause moments of anxiety or even panic. It is usually preferable to be open and honest and for practitioners to confess any bamboozled moments, requesting time to rethink a response or to clear the head. Clients invariably understand if the helper makes a mistake, such as forgetting a piece of information about the client, losing their place in the process or becoming stuck for words. It demonstrates respect for clients when the practitioner is transparent about any struggles to be empathic and competent. It is more genuine and 'real' to admit mistakes and to correct these in full sight of clients. On occasions this may mean saying something like *'I think I was not very clear just now – let me try to say that differently'* when it is apparent that the client is confused about what has just been said. It is far less demanding, in both the learning phase and during work in the human service field, to admit to lapses of concentration or confidence, rather than pretending to be perfectly in charge, especially when there is confusion and anxiety beneath the surface.

Key points about concluding the interview

➤ In concluding it is important to affirm the client as this may colour further outcomes

➤ Ask to what extent the client's goals, defined at its beginning, have been achieved

➤ As part of the conclusion, provide a final summary of the client's achievements

➤ The interpreted interview requires carefully crafted conclusions, conveyed through the interpreter

➤ Interviews concluded with courtesy and care help clients leave with increased self-esteem

CHAPTER OVERVIEW

In summary then, this chapter has reviewed the importance of active and purposeful work within a framework of empathic responding, including guiding the client to focus on a range of relevant issues by using smooth transitions. The tension between empathy and direction was discussed, especially the intersection of client 'resistance' into this set of issues. Managing the balance between empathy and direction requires planning and effective interview management. When the practitioner demonstrates these processes and continues to profile reflective and empathic responses, most clients feel safe in the competent support offered and cooperate to share better information. This text now moves on to the important process of *deliberately* focusing paraphrases in such a way as to encourage the client to become more aware of their behaviours and reactions and to gradually accept responsibility for deciding how to make some positive changes in how they manage life's challenges.

CHAPTER 6

Goal and Action Work with Clients

By way of review, so far skills that are central to responding empathically have been described as acknowledging the *feelings, situations* and *behaviours* of the client, in ways that are meaningful, coherent and focused on the client's current issues. An effective strengths perspective has been noted as a key process of affirming clients' self-esteem and letting clients know we see them as experts in their own lives. In addition, a set of processes about managing the direction and flow of the interview have been described. Even when the interviewer consistently manages all these skills and processes, some clients require additional help to overcome entrenched self–defeating patterns of thought or obsession about negative aspects of their life. As well, clients struggle with lack of motivation and need encouragement to think about how to work on *small steps* to move towards achieving their goals. This chapter has these matters as its focus.

As a first stage in this set of processes, it is essential to focus paraphrases strategically to direct client's thinking and conceptual processes. Sometimes this is also about helping clients draw back from negative self-talk. But first it is important to underline that in beginning to focus on goals, the structure of paraphrases is the absolute basis of goal-focused talk. Goals come from clients being helped to identify their *current behaviours* (by the interviewer clearly stating the clients' 'behaviours' as part of reflections and paraphrases). Some behaviours are dysfunctional and when these are clearly stated and the client accepts that things need to change, this becomes the basis for change where clients are learning ways to manage their life more functionally.

Clients' feelings or emotions, perceptions of situations and of their own behaviour, all need to be expressed *with causal links* in paraphrases to demonstrate the relationship between these in client's lives and to establish the foundation for clear and specific goal talk. The interviewer who has managed their paraphrases with deliberate and purposeful focus will have maximized the client's understanding of their feelings *as differentiated* from the *situations* and certainly from *their behaviours*.

For this to take place the following elements need to be consistently included in paraphrases:

- Reflections of accurate feelings – how they *feel* now – their emotions
- Descriptions of situations or experiences – what's *happening to them/around them* – in concise and accurate terms
- Descriptions of clients' behaviours, actions/reactions – what they are *doing* now – expressed clearly and accurately

These all help the client to understand the differences between *feelings*, *situations* and *behaviours/actions* when they are linked and combined in coherent and clear paraphrases.

BUT – to do this, the practitioner, and in time the client, *must be able to differentiate between feelings, situations and behaviours* also. Essentially, preparing clients for goal-focused work is based on crystal-clear identification of behaviours in which the client currently engages and which are contributing to their situation. These then become the focus for further goal-directed discussion.

Importance of the behaviour element in preparing for goal-focused work

Accurately reflecting their behaviours can be confronting to some clients, especially if dysfunctional behaviours are the focus. So for this reason, it is best to delay focusing on behaviour patterns that are dysfunctional until a firm platform of trust and understanding has been established. However it is appropriate to focus on *positive behaviours* as soon as these become apparent in work with clients. When issues have been fully explored and the client seems ready to start to focus honestly on their current behaviour patterns, then it is possible to begin to name less functional behaviours as a prelude to focusing on goals.

Forms of client behaviour

Behaviour reflections (or the behaviour component in paraphrases) can focus on a range of different client behaviours as mentioned in Chapter 3.

As described, understanding these differences (between inside and outside behaviours and between feelings and behaviours) is absolutely essential in helping clients identify their current behaviours and to refine and strengthen their identification of goals as a basis for solution-focused change.

Visible, external behaviours or actions

In the course of a day, everyone engages in a range of external behaviours. For instance, we talk, run, sit quietly, yell, go to lectures, cry, miss tutorials, eat lunch, skip breakfast and so on – and these are all *overt* behaviours that can be easily noticed, by other people for instance. These are things the client does too – maybe to other people or things – e.g. talks, shouts, hits, hugs, or otherwise acts towards others in the situation e.g. 'you shouted at Tom and then stormed out'. These are behaviours that others could observe or which could be observed reasonably easily – or recorded even, if a video camera was running and focused on what the client was doing.

But we also do some things that are less able to be noticed – we talk to ourselves, obsess about what we said yesterday, imagine what we might do or say tomorrow, tell ourselves we are stupid – and so on. These are things that we do on the inside and which are also very powerful shapers of our external behaviours.

Internalized behaviours

Internalized behaviours are things people do *on the inside* or *to self* and these are not so overt or readily observable. These often include self-talk, obsessed thinking and self-directed actions which are much less clear to you or others and would not be able to be recorded on a video camera or, if they were, would require further explanation to understand their significance.

- Internal processes may be self-talk – e.g. *'you keep telling yourself he hates you'*, or *'you are going over and over in your head what happened'* or for a more positive focus *'you are pushing away the black thoughts'*.
- Some internal behaviours may have visible signs – but are symbolic of other things going on e.g. *'You ate a whole block of chocolate last night'*.
- Interpretive statements about these 'symbolic' behaviours are best avoided – e.g. it is not a good idea to say *'Your hostile relationship with your father*

means you drink yourself into oblivion every night to blot him out' – as this may be quite wrong or they may not want to discuss it in this context. Likewise, judgemental statements are not useful either in discussing these internalized behaviours e.g. *'You drink too much'* or *'You pigged out on chocolate'.* These statements will assist clients neither to focus productively on their current behaviours nor to work at changing these for the better.

However it is useful to express responses in a way that helps clients to see their dysfunctional patterns of behaviour by naming these clearly and objectively. This is especially so when it is apparent that clients' negative self-talk is the basis of self-defeating symbolic acts, as this is the beginning of a focus on helping clients to shift their self-talk as a first step in changing both their internal and external or symbolic behaviour.

Key points about internal and external behaviours

➤ External behaviour is action carried out by clients and which is able to be seen by others or recorded in some way such as on a video or DVD

➤ Internal behaviour is less visible, and is often related to client self-talk

➤ Some behaviour is symbolic of things going on inside the client's mind and needs to be carefully understood and not interpreted

➤ It is usually best to positively frame responses about behaviour but sometimes dysfunctional behaviour needs to be honestly identified

---

Reframing clients' negative thinking

Self-supporting internal client processes that involve positive thought patterns are to be actively encouraged, as opposed to negative self-talk, which is often at the basis of entrenched patterns of low self-esteem. A focus on the development of positive self-talk may in time lead to more effective behaviour patterns. Positive motivational frames also mean the client's energy is tapped and the life flow is redirected. However, in asking clients to question their ingrained self-perceptions, interviewers will frequently encounter resistance and will need intelligence and creativity to motivate clients who are stuck in self-defeating cycles of thought and behaviour. People cling to negative self-images, rebuilding these daily through their self-talk and it is clearly very important to understand this to work with clients in this area. At this point it is important to stress here that even if more direct, worker-initiated processes are required to help clients to move out of their stuck positions, these should only be applied within the usual processes of empathic exploration which of itself engenders a level of client self-challenge.

As mentioned previously, it is essential that the interviewer actively listens for positive aspects of the client's life and focuses on these to encourage the client to recognize their own capabilities and strengths. For this to happen, clients may need to be actively supported to reframe their thinking about some issues, especially if they are stuck in self-defeating thought patterns. Hutchins and Vaught (1997, p. 238) suggest that clients may need help to recognize negative internalized conversations and this is important as these can continue to interfere with a client's motivation and focus on goals and action work.

Recognizing patterns in clients' thinking

Hutchins and Vaught (1997, pp. 31–37) describe four patterns of clients' thinking that frame their views and colour their approaches to managing life's challenges. These are related to the previous material about paraphrasing and the focus on feelings, situations and behaviours. In unveiling clients' thinking patterns, especially negative and defeatist ones, the ability of the interviewer to discriminate between these in their talk is essential. Each of the patterns below as described by Hutchins and Vaught (1997) demonstrates the link between the paraphrase components of *feeling, situation* and *behaviour*.

Thinking (about situation) + feelings

When a client demonstrates this pattern in their self-talk, thinking and narrative then they are likely to be insightful, curious and clever with strong feelings about situations and people. They may be thoughtful and caring and sympathetic toward others in trouble (Hutchins and Vaught 1997, pp. 32, 33). They may also be passionate about lots of things, but frustrated at different times however and have difficulty in putting plans into action. Organized planning is not their strong suit as they are often unable to decide on courses of action and may get caught up in emotional dithering. Clients with this pattern often need help in identifying behaviours/goals, in determining action approaches and following through on these. In working with clients with this pattern of thinking it is very important to focus on behavioural elements in the paraphrasing work and then later to take particular care in structuring small behavioural steps with effective reinforcement structured into the program of action.

Feeling + action/behaviour

The client with this pattern in their communication style may display a trigger reaction between feeling and behaviour. They may react emotionally, taking heroic if premature actions at times, combined sometimes with being warm, open and trusting towards others. But at other times they may also be impulsive to the point of own or other's risk and consequently they may spend much energy making up for impulsive actions (Hutchins and Vaught 1997, p. 33). Note the absence of thinking impacts generally on their goal achievement. This person may need help in identifying their thoughts about the situation, help in understanding others' actions and the separation between own feelings and behaviour. Some need support in increasing their impulse control. Clients with this feeling/action pattern may also seem out of control in their lives, displaying aggression, addictive patterns, impulsiveness, poor planning and the tendency to be overly emotional. Paraphrases that emphasize the separation between feelings and behaviour are essential here.

Thinking + action/behaviours

This person knows how to plan and carry through ideas to completion and they may be insightful and persistent. They lack an appreciation of own and others' feelings and so may be impatient with others and lack compassion or overpower others in their desire to make things happen (Hutchins and Vaught 1997, p. 34). The low importance of feelings for clients with this pattern means they may need particular help in noticing and naming their feelings. Consequently paraphrases that emphasize their feelings as they relate to the situation are important. Clients with this profile may also tend to avoid feelings and be super-rational. Sometimes these are people who are especially unaware of the impact of their own actions on others or do not notice or care about others' feelings. Help in becoming more aware of own and others' feelings is offered through the consistent application of paraphrases focusing on emotions.

Thinking + feeling + acting

Balance of all three aspects means this sort of person seems thoughtful, understanding, insightful of own and others' feelings and can see all points of view (Hutchins and Vaught 1997, p. 35). They are also able to carry through goals to action, after due consideration and planning. At times clients with all three qualities well balanced as in this pattern may need encouragement to trust their judgement and to move on their plans. They can be cautious in acting compared with other types mentioned here, especially the more impulsive action/feeling individuals.

Hutchins and Vaught (1997) provide a useful analysis for considering client needs in terms of the balance of their focus on feelings, situations and/or behaviours. This may be important in terms of how interviewers respond to them during the early stages of their narrative but these features come into even higher relief during points where goal talk begins to occur. Targeted use of paraphrases, where components of feeling, situation and behaviour are deliberately combined for maximum positive effect, requires good control over what is included in responses, highlighting the need to be deliberate and purposeful in responding in every way.

Key points about clients' thinking patterns

➤ Effective paraphrasing helps clients identify the differences between feeling, situations and behaviours – and this enables them to take greater control of their thoughts and behaviours

➤ Patterns of clients' thinking may determine the appropriate focus of paraphrasing work

➤ These patterns refer to relationships between thinking, feeling and acting and the need to be quite purposeful in identifying these

➤ Clients with a thinking/feeling pattern often need help in identifying behaviours/goals, in determining action approaches and following through on these

➤ Clients with a feeling/acting pattern need help in understanding the difference between feelings and behaviour and support in increasing their impulse control

➤ Clients with a thinking/acting pattern may need help in noticing and naming their feelings and being more aware of the emotional impact of own actions on others

➤ Clients with a balance of thinking/feeling and acting are able to carry through goals from planning to action, although they may seem cautious compared with other thinking patterns

Helping clients with blind spots

Assisting clients to attain a balance of thinking, feeling and acting in their lives sometimes means, following the establishment of trust, focusing on what appear to be their blind spots. Egan (2007, p. 149) discusses the nature of what he calls *blind spots* – that is, 'things we fail to see or choose to ignore' of which clients can be largely unaware or choose not let into their conscious thought. Some of these unexamined patterns may drag the client down into a maelstrom of negativity and hopelessness in trying to manage their life, robbing them of energy, motivation and the ability to achieve their goals. Egan (2007, pp. 149–152) identifies four general areas of psychological blind spots that people commonly experience. The first of these is *simple unawareness*, which refers to some clients who never seem to think much at all about their own internal processes, including unconscious negative self-talk and self-defeating thoughts. *Failure to think things through* may lead to impulsive and ill-considered acts that often cause more trouble for self and others. *Self-deception* involves a more deliberate, though not always fully conscious, turning away from self-knowledge and of defending the self against this knowledge – to keep their lives and others under control. *Choosing to stay in the dark* is a kind of evasiveness game of denial where a person consciously avoids looking at difficult things in their life. Finally, *knowing, not caring and failing to see consequences* refers to clients who 'do not fully understand or appreciate the degree to which they are choosing their own misery' (Egan 2007, p. 151) and this may be associated with appearing to make no effort at all to deal with life's challenges.

Egan (2007, pp. 152–156) explores a range of issues that may assist clients to overcome their blind spots. He suggest that sometimes clients may need to be challenged about self-limiting internal and external behaviours, gently confronted about discrepancies, dishonesties and about unused strengths and resources. Some of these processes sound fairly negative and hard on the client. Successful challenging of the client's unused strengths, skills and capacities however is a central process in a strengths approach. It is about reshaping the client's self-image from one that is self-defeating into one that is more positive. Strategies can include asking the client to imagine unused opportunities, to state their problems as solvable and to gradually move away from self-limiting views. In time, this may mean chipping away at the everyday self-limitations they impose on their experience of life and, in turn, increasing positive self-esteem.

Egan (2007, pp. 152–154) suggests that practitioners offer little benefit to clients if they are not able to challenge their blind spots effectively. Where possible, interviewers should encourage client self-challenge rather than confronting and challenging the client. In doing so, the interviewer aims to be tentative but not apologetic, to be specific, to focus on the client's unused strengths and successes more than weaknesses, to respect the client's values and overall to deal honestly, caringly and creatively with client defensiveness.

Interviewers especially need to resist their own tendencies to become vague and theoretical with clients when discussing these patterns of thought, blind spots and patterns of external behaviour or internal self-talk. Instead, the need is to remain primarily focused on concrete aspects such as the client's behaviours and skills and to work collaboratively to identify *small steps* for the client to move positively towards managing life's issues.

Key points about managing clients' blind spots

➤ Blind spots may be dysfunctions about which the client is unaware, deceives self about, chooses not to look at, or just does not care about

➤ Helping clients with blind spots may mean challenging them about self-limiting behaviours

➤ This may also mean confronting them gently about unused strengths and resources

➤ Challenging clients to see their strengths is a key feature of a strengths approach

Focusing on goals and managing client change processes

Not all interviews focus on goal-setting and change processes. Goal and action strategies will be of primary interest to practitioners who are working in contexts where there is the opportunity to see the client through a process of change whether it is short-term or long-term. In some settings, interviews with a client may take place over several different sessions spread over weeks or even months. In others the process may be more intense and the change process may be part of one or two sessions. Sometimes it is less likely that interviewers will see the same client more than once. With some clients in certain settings, it may be that there is no commitment to work together to focus on goals and change, related to how they manage their life situations. This diversity means only some readers of this book may see the following material as directly relevant to their current and/or future interviewing practice. Consequently, this is a relatively brief overview of goal-setting and action processes. I would encourage those working in areas where these processes are a more central part of their work, to view this chapter as introductory in nature and to seek further reading and practice in these skills and processes.

The empathic skills applied in early parts of the interview process remain strongly applicable in examining goal setting and action or change approaches. As well, emphasis on clients' strengths and coping goals remains applicable across all stages of work. In reference to solution and change strategies, the focus is on clients' coping goals as the task becomes one of helping them to locate small steps that support change whilst holding to that which is important in their lives, both culturally and personally.

Goal directed thinking – or not!

'Goal and action strategies' is really just fancy terminology for *wanting something* and *understanding what has to be done to get it*. Put simply, the practitioner supports clients to find answers to two questions – *What do I want?* and *What do I have to do to get what I want?* Goal setting or planning, focused on the near or more distant future, is a normal human function and is not a particularly new idea for many people. Most individuals set goals at some point in their lives, committing themselves to future achievements. However, not everyone understands how to focus their efforts to best attain these. Sometimes individual's goals are less well-formed ideas that float in and out of full consciousness, as other things that seem more important or urgent take over. Many people have few really overtly expressed goals to guide their energy in life and so they plod or lurch from disaster to emergency through their lives. Life defines what happens to them and they wonder why they feel powerless, or resentful or dissatisfied. As John Lennon sang, 'Life is what happens to you while you're busy making other plans.' Some individuals feel deeply resentful because they never seem to get what they want. It is usually the case that if an individual keeps doing what they have always done, then they will keep getting what they already have. They need to do different things to make the change from how 'life happens to them' to taking charge and making things happen. In the interview setting, some clients seem better able to express what they want and need when they are listened to and responded to empathically. But many need particular assistance to understand how to attain their goals. It is often news to clients – and a relief when they understand it – that attaining goals is a manageable process entailing *small steps* along the path and that these *baby steps* are pieces of behaviour within their power to achieve. Without understanding these processes, many will go on seeing change as hopelessly out of their reach.

Internal thought processes and goal-focused work

Clear ideas about steps and processes are more likely to lead to goal success. Goal achievement in turn engenders self-efficacy and a sense of personal control that leads to the likelihood of further goal success. It is important however, to understand that client goal achievement is often strongly related to or even dependent on internal processes. For example, it is apparent that the qualities of resourcefulness and internal persistence are related to goal achievement in a chicken-and-egg way. This is just another way of saying that belief in one's levels of power and personal control over life events taps into internal self-talk and to locus of control. Locus of control is a term coined by Rotter in 1973 (Myers 1993, p. 104) and has been expanded by Bandura (1989 in Myers 1993, p. 107) to the concept of 'self-efficacy'. Both terms – locus of control and self-efficacy – refer to the extent to which clients believe they are in charge of their achievements in life and in turn feel in control of attaining further outcomes. Myers (1993, p. 104) notes that 'those who see themselves as internally controlled are more likely to do well in school, successfully stop smoking, wear seat belts, practice birth control, deal with marital problems directly, make lots of money, and delay instant gratification in order to achieve long-term goals' (Myers 1993, p. 104). Who would not want to be this way? Individuals with an *internal* locus of control believe that events result primarily from their own behaviour and actions, whereas those with an *external* locus of control believe that powerful others, fate or luck determines events and outcomes – or that life *just happens to them*. Those with an internal locus of control have well defined strategies aimed at influencing outcomes, tend to exhibit positive energy and believe they have power to influence life's directions; they are also more likely to assume that their efforts will be successful. Such individuals are also active in seeking information and knowledge concerning their situation than are those with an external locus of control.

The positive impact of well-formed goals

It is apparent from the preceding discussion about locus of control that people who are good goal setters often possess more self-control, persistence and energy, enabling them to achieve their goals. They are therefore also less likely to need help from practitioners in the human services. Consequently, interviewers may not find many clients with these characteristics. Many clients seeking support from a range of agencies are more likely to have an external locus of control, lower energy, a history of poor goal achievement and not much faith in their own power. In working with these clients, practitioners need to be really clear about discussing goals as achievable – through defining and following small steps – *baby steps* – as this helps to build their optimism. It also means keeping a focus on clients' positive skills and coping goals and demonstrating understanding of their narrative about life. This means noticing the real achievements of the client – however small – and focusing on these as a means of building self-esteem. Realistic self-esteem based on personal qualities and achievements means clients can identify what they have done well and begin to feel more in control of future outcomes.

In beginning a goal process by focusing on small steps, clients feel more energized and in time develop more faith in their own power to change. Effective goal and change focused talk, guided by a competent interviewer in the first instance, provides clients with a sense of direction and a stronger belief in their ability to control own outcomes generally. It is true that many clients have intractably hard lives and will find it difficult to make changes that may be in part dependent on other people's cooperation. For this reason, goal talk needs to focus on own behaviours, thoughts and feelings and how to begin to change these – not those of other people. Changes in other people in the client's life may result as spin-offs, based on the whirlpool effect when a client begins to take control of changing their own behaviours – and this is a bonus.

However, even if nothing else changes, when clients learn to manage own feelings and behavioural responses to people and situations, they feel more in control of their lives and experience an increase in self-esteem – and this sets off other positive change.

Goal formation and locating personal solutions is hard work for clients and it is vital that the interviewer recognizes this and affirms clients for their efforts. Genuine affirmation and competent goal-directed work with clients can mean they leave sessions with higher self-esteem, a greater sense of self-control and with stronger hope for the future. This is about consistent empathic responding that builds up to a focus on small behaviours – baby steps within the client's reach and which they soon see can build into something bigger.

Well-formed goals

The qualities of well-formed goals are discussed more fully by De Jong and Berg (2008, pp. 77–83). Goal-focused work is part of a strengths-focused approach in working with clients. To be effective, the areas of focus must be important to the client and formed from the client's frame of reference. This means well-formed goals belong to the client, not the interviewer. As well, goals must be expressed in terms of behavioural changes in the client – both external and internal – and able to be noticed by others who share the client's life. Well-formed goals take account of situational factors and are expressed in terms of the presence of *desirable behaviours*. Effective goals usually *do not focus on behaviours expressed in the negative* – like **not** feeling depressed or on **stopping** day-dreaming. In other words the goal is focused instead on what the client *will* do. The client might be asked to focus on what someone would *notice them doing* if they were feeling less depressed – such as going for a walk every day, having a coffee with a friend on the weekend or eating breakfast regularly. Then the task is about focusing on this behaviour – in small behaviourally focused steps (*baby steps* – that can be achieved tomorrow, this week, next week).

Egan (2007, pp. 250, 251) also describes four empowering functions of well-formed goals. He suggests that effective goals need to:

- Focus the 'client's attention and action' by helping them identify something they really want;
- Mobilize clients' 'energy and effort' through the focus of new possibilities;

- Motivate the client's 'search for strategies to accomplish them' by encouraging divergent thinking and focusing on ways to get what they want;
- Increase clients' persistence – especially when the focus is in on small, achievable and specific behaviours that are fairly immediately possible.

Keep goal talk simple

Always in discussing goals – it is important to focus on *beginning steps* or **baby steps** and *not on final solutions* as stressed also by De Jong and Berg (2008, pp. 88, 81). Effective goals focus on a client's specific small behaviours with time frames for each of these. These goals are also *concrete, behavioural and measurable*. Finally, they must be both *realistic* but as well *sufficiently challenging* for the client to maintain energy and focus.

The use of empathic skills remains central in encouraging the client to express ideas and suggestions for own goal directions. In keeping with the principles of a strengths perspective, interviewers regularly affirm clients for the hard work involved in forming good goals and compliment them for the positive work they have completed throughout the process.

Key points about setting effective goals

➤ Goal setting or planning is a normal human function

➤ Goal achievement increases personal control and the likelihood of further goal success

➤ In interviewing, a successful solution-focused process is based on effective goals

➤ Effective goals belong to the client, emerge from their experiences and may be assisted by brainstorming

➤ Clients are energized by goal-focused work and a belief in their own power to change

➤ Effective goals are based on a view of small 'baby' steps, not on final solutions

➤ Effective goals are behavioural, concrete, measurable, realistic and challenging

Goal bridges and the miracle question

De Jong and Berg (2008, pp. 83–89) suggest that a *miracle question* approach can provide a kind of bridge for some clients who really struggle to imagine a life unlike their present one and who need additional help in imagining a better set of circumstances.

The miracle question looks something like this: 'Suppose a miracle happened, and you woke up tomorrow morning and the problem that brought you here is solved. What would be different about your behaviour in your everyday life?' This is a particular technique, using a positive imagination-based perspective, to 'unstick' clients. With this approach, the client is encouraged to think outside the square, to imagine a better world and then to work backwards from this, to specify the *small first steps* towards this 'miracle'. This process is surrounded with positive affirmation and a focus on the client's strengths. Also vital in the success of this approach is the development of well-formed *positive goals*, that behaviours are things to do – not to avoid doing – as described by De Jong and Berg (2008, pp. 79–80).

Moving towards a solution entails taking the ideas coming out of the miracle question (or other positive goal-directed talk and/or brainstorming), and thinking about these in terms of small 'baby' steps. Reality checks need to be used to ensure these are achievable. Some steps may be set as homework tasks and the client may be encouraged to think of ways to reward self for small steps accomplished.

As a kind of inoculation against negative self-talk, clients are affirmed by the interviewer throughout all sessions and as they leave. Many may also need to be encouraged to use positive imagery in between sessions to maintain their motivation. Some interviewers may wish to arrange for telephone or email connection with clients in between interview sessions to provide interim affirmation and encouragement.

Brainstorming strategies

Brainstorming a range of strategies from way-out to realistic helps to broaden the client's views about possibilities and stimulates lateral thinking and creativity. The process is one of finding how many ways there may be to approach a goal. The process needs to include a review of the resources the client either has or needs to acquire. This includes social support as well as more material resources and some focus on the working knowledge or skills the client has currently or needs to acquire.

Searching for effective strategies by using *brainstorming* encourages clients to think beyond the square in terms of possible approaches to working on a goal. For example, when the client knows what the issues are they need to work on, but actual strategies are unclear, then Egan (2007, pp. 259–263) notes the effectiveness of brainstorming as a way to suspend judgement – both clients' and interviewers' – about these. The idea is that the client has a goal in mind and is encouraged to consider a wide and wild range of possibilities as ways to achieve this goal. These may be quite crazy or way-out things as sometimes a crazy possibility sparks off further good ideas. So if the issue is one of an overweight client *losing weight* with a focus on dieting, then the range of brainstormed strategies might go something like this:

- *Fast completely for a month*
- *Eat only apples until I get to my desired weight*
- *Have stomach stapled*
- *Give away all food currently in my cupboard and fridge*
- *Establish a web site where I publicly record everything I eat every day*
- *Ask a thin friend to move in with me and to control and record what I eat*

After the list has been brainstormed and perhaps written on a whiteboard or large sheet of paper, then the process is one of discussing each idea to assess it according to its value – in terms of things like achievability, cost or other factors important to the client. As well, some of the items might be able to be combined into a more effective approach.

In working with a client who wants to give up smoking, a similar range of strategies might be brainstormed.

These might include the following range:

- *go to a health farm*
- *cold turkey*
- *undergo hypnosis*
- *gradually cut down one cigarette a day until all have been given up*
- *use nicotine patches alone or in combination with other strategies.*

The process of brainstorming may not always be declared as such to the client but could just be a gentle suggestion about freeing up thinking about how to approach a goal area. The major purpose of brainstorming is to bring forth suggestions about possible ways forward not previously considered by the client or the interviewer.

Best-fit approach to selecting strategies

Egan (2007, pp. 309–317) discusses 'best-fit strategies' which encourage the client to address which strategies fit best in reference to personal values and situational circumstances that cannot be changed (realism). In choosing the best strategy, all circumstances surrounding the client's situation need to be considered, including a review of resources and personal skills. Egan (2007, pp. 313–314) describes the use of a *Balance-Sheet* in helping clients to choose strategies. In summary this involves the consideration of ideas like these:

- How will a particular (brainstormed) strategy benefit me? Or others I care about?
- What are the costs of this strategy to me? To others I care about?
- How acceptable are these costs to me? To others I care about?
- How unacceptable are these costs to me? To others?

A *balance-sheet* method may be employed to analyse benefits and costs or the acceptability of a particular strategy with reference to current factors in the client's life. This strategy is then linked to action – to a set of *baby steps* toward the goal. The interviewer needs to remain vigilant and look out for wishful thinking, playing it safe, avoiding pain, and other avoidance tactics used by clients and workers to deflect the focus from change.

Key points about miracle questions, brainstorming and best-fit strategies

➤ Employing the miracle question to imagine possible futures may 'unstick' clients

➤ Affirming clients provides a kind of inoculation against negative self-talk

➤ Empathic skills are maintained to encourage the client to focus on own goal directions

➤ Brainstorming may help to define new perspectives about goals

➤ A balance sheet approach considers effects and outcomes of selected approaches

Turning goals into solution-focused action – the path to change

All goal-focused talk and the search for appropriate action strategies and approaches need to fit the client and to be supported by the use of consistent use of empathic responses. The most effective goals and action strategies focus on *beginning steps*, not on trying to fix multi-factorial problems through a single plan focused on big, wide-reaching goals. The focus for work is always *beginnings* or *first steps*, which are the first moves towards a solution. This entails taking one of the goal areas and determining through discussion with the client the small steps that will be both challenging enough but feasible in terms of achievement. Then it is a matter of deciding what is worked on first, second and so on.

The importance of small 'baby' steps towards change

De Jong and Berg (2008, pp. 80, 81) view final solutions as elusive and inadvisable as a focus for looking at client change – and this is a key idea. Clients miss this point very often and may pressure the interviewer in human service settings for immediate relief for their life pain. Being able to identify *small steps* that are achievable – *one by one* – helps to address this pressure as it provides a definable path toward change – with distinct steps that are achievable within a short period of time.

Case study – Jo's plan of baby steps toward change

Jo wants to increase her physical activity and to become fitter as an overall goal. She identifies increasing her activity and expertise in surfing as a sub-goal. She accepts this is just a small part of her overall goal but believes it is a useful place to begin. The interviewer suggests the action step process begins by Jo identifying *benefits* and *rewards* for focusing on this sub-goal first and from achieving it – as additional motivation. Jo identifies the following:

- I love surfing – I know I will enjoy it
- It will help me to build fitness
- It's sociable – something I can do with my friends
- It's a skill and mastering it would give me a real sense of achievement.

Then following this, the next stage entails helping Jo to identify specific staged steps involved in working on this goal PLUS target dates for each stage:

- Ask Mum and Dad to pay for three surfing lessons as part of my birthday present – target date: Ask them tonight
- Join the local board riders club – target date next week: by Tuesday 2 May
- Go out with Dan (brother) who is good at surfing and get him to give me some tips – target date: This weekend 6/7 May
- Go surfing at least three times a week for the next three weeks (at least two mornings before work and once on the weekend) – target date: begin 8th May

The nitty-gritty (baby steps to do – this week):

TONIGHT:

- Talk to Mum and Dad about financial help with my surfing lessons.
- Ask Dan about going surfing with him.

TOMORROW:

- Ring the local board riders club and find out about membership.

WEDNESDAY:

- Book my surfing lessons for weekends over the next six weeks.

By providing a range of other *support, information, instruction and suggestions* new information may be presented to the client in this *small step* focused action phase through a range of processes such as skills rehearsal, clinical or medical tests to assess baseline fitness or health or other processes to support targeted action steps. Finally, some *directive processes,* may be used where suggestions of approaches or supportive resources provided by the practitioner can reinforce clients in their resolve to take steps towards their goals. In brief, turning plans into action means focusing on clear small steps that will bring the client some fairly immediate results and will help them take further steps towards overall goal achievement.

During the goal and action phases the interviewer maintains the use of reflective responses that encourage the client to generate a narrative about possible solutions, goals and small steps. During these goal and action focused processes, interviewers sometimes influence and encourage the client to be specific, creative, to try new things and to explore a range of alternatives. The interviewer affirms and reinforces the client for thinking of clear, small behaviours and for designing baby steps to reach their goals.

A formal or informal contract may be defined – who will do what, by when, under what conditions and so on. There may be a clear definition of what the client will do (baby steps, by when and so on) but it may also list what the interviewer will do, such as follow up via phone or email to support the client in dealing with the pressures involved in managing change in their lives. Such contracts are best kept to a short-term basis to allow for review and feedback as the change process occurs.

In working with clients, most human service practitioners hope to see them take a bit more control of their lives and to find solutions to their problems. Sometimes this involves the interviewer encouraging the client to 'have a go', to be more courageous in attempting change and to have more hope in there being some positive outcomes. This requires a fine differentiation between motivating, challenging and supporting clients – and avoidance of advice-driven approaches that erode clients' self-motivation and decision-making power.

Sometimes however, clients may seem to have lost hope about everything – and are so far down and so disengaged that they do not seem to want anything strongly enough even to talk about forming small steps towards the goal. When clients are unable to focus on change, then approaches that directly build their motivation first may be more beneficial.

Key steps in applying an action plan

➤ Develop the plan by formulating *the goal area for focus*

➤ Select *a sub-goal* for initial focus

➤ Name and sequence the baby steps: 'What do I do first? What do I do second?

➤ Break these right down in term of daily tasks and design an overview plan or stairway

➤ Agree on realistic timelines for each step on the stairway

➤ Identify resources/reinforcements to support/reward each step in the sequence

➤ Summarize the 'contract' – the steps, the timeline, resources and rewards

Motivational interviewing approaches

Clients who are not ready to take responsibility for change in their own lives are often viewed as having motivational problems. Those working with dependent or addicted clients in particular will find the motivational approach of Miller and Rollnick (2002) highly applicable. Addictive behaviours are not confined to alcohol or other drug use and abuse by the way. Addiction is, as Freud (1948) describes it, the seductive and self-defeating pull of neurotic behaviours, as cited by Miller and Rollnick in their 1991 edition (page ix). Some people are addicted to *food and over-eating*, to *relationships* that seem toxic for them for instance, or to other self-macerating processes, such as out-of-control gambling and a range of other varied obsessions.

Miller and Rollnick (2002) suggest that working with addicted people of all kinds is about understanding their ambivalence (I want to change/ I don't want to change/I am afraid of what will happen to me if I keep doing it/ I am afraid of who I will become if I do change). So success in motivating clients is about helping them find the courage to be stronger, happier and more in control of their lives. They suggest that motivational processes are absolutely vital with some clients to focus a client's thinking on the balance between costs and benefits and of change versus no change. As a client's attitude towards change is a combination of their strength of desire for the change and the confidence they have in their own ability to make it (Miller and Rollnick 2002, p. 54), the first process in working with some clients is one of assessing their motivational state. Have they begun to contemplate change? Have they formed some sort of determination to change? If they are committed to change, what is their continuing level of ambivalence and do they feel confident to manage it?

Phases of motivational work

There are two phases in Miller and Rollnick's (2002) motivational approach. The first is focused on *building motivation for change* and the second on *strengthening the client's confidence and commitment*. The work of the first phase depends on how advanced the client is in terms of being motivated to make changes. The motivational approach of Miller and Rollnick is described by Di Clemente and Velasquez (2002, p. 202) as an 'excellent counselling style to use with clients who are in the early stages' meaning pre-contemplation and contemplation, as '*Pre-contemplators* do not want to be lectured or given "action" techniques when they are not ready to change'.

A framework for assessing motivational states

This is suggested by Di Clemente and Velasquez (2002, pp. 201–213), entailing five stages that may be cyclical in nature as the client moves backwards and forwards between these.

1. **Pre–contemplation** refers to clients who have limited awareness and see little reason to change. These clients are most in need of help in building motivation.
2. **Contemplation** is where clients have become aware of issues related to their situation. Here the client is beginning to think about change but needs help to decide what this may mean and to make a clear decision about it.
3. **Preparation** means the client has accepted the need to change and is well motivated although they may need help in planning the steps and keeping focused on the change process.
4. **Action** is when the client devotes good energy to behaving differently and follows the steps, although they may still need some support to get through early difficulties and to consolidate new behaviours.
5. **Maintenance** means the client has achieved their goal, is working on sustaining long-term change but is not yet free of struggle and needs some ongoing support to avoid or manage lapses.

These principles are maintained throughout the working relationship with the client although the overall process of motivational interviewing happens in two phases. The first is focused on *locating and building up motivation* (for those who are pre-contemplators). The second phase is focused on *planning goals, deciding on action strategies and supporting the client to change* (for those now committed and ready to change). The practitioner maintains reflective skills and motivational principles throughout both phases.

Phase I – Building motivation for change

The first phase is focused on assessing and building the client's motivation for change. If clients are pre-contemplative or just starting to contemplate change in any realistic way, the interviewing task is one of resolving clients' ambivalence. The assumption is that a client with low motivational levels *is ambivalent* about change and so this first phase is about avoiding the traps (and roadblocks as discussed in Chapter 2) that will increase client ambivalence. These may include the question-answer trap, confrontation-denial trap, expert trap, labelling trap, premature advice trap and blaming trap (Miller and Rollnick 2002, pp. 55–63).

Rolling with resistance (Wagner and Sanchez 2002, p. 293) is an attitude of mind where the interviewer avoids head-to-head confrontation – even deliberately ducking it, as ambivalent clients will inevitably argue back. Forcing a client into a position where they need to defend themselves breeds further ambivalence and resistance. Likewise, labelling clients as alcoholic or addicted for instance is unproductive – but clients sometimes diagnose themselves or may wish to. The trick is for the worker to encourage the activation of critical thinking in the client. Of course, this would only be appropriate after a sense of trust has been established. With some clients, diagnostic tests of fitness, liver and heart profiles or other health screening may be useful as a source of independent feedback, but discussing the results of these needs to be managed with sensitivity. The whole idea is to help the client to find his/her own reasons to make changes and to feel committed to doing so.

Early strategies also include staying with the client through the strategic use of Open-ended questions, Affirming, Reflective listening and Summarizing – represented in the acronym OARS by Miller and Rollnick (2002, p. 65). These responses, described fully in previous chapters, are key skills in eliciting self-motivational statements that help clients to look more honestly and courageously at their life now, before and in the future. Questions like 'Describe what you were doing when things were going well for you? What has changed?' may help to facilitate this self-understanding. This links to De Jong and Berg's (2008) coping goals focus. In Miller and Rollnick's first phase, goal talk operates as a kind of litmus test of motivation. If the client is committed at the start, then Phase 1 may only entail the establishment of a trusting professional relationship and the gaining of a mutual understanding about the issues. Motivational interviewing is empathic in nature but as well it is 'consciously directive' according to Miller and Rollnick (2002, p. 25). They stress, as have I previously, that empathy is not a passive process but rather involves actively selecting what to attend to from the client's narrative, gradually angling to focus on the client's current behaviours. Miller and Rollnick (2002, p. 25) also note that the motivational interviewer 'elicits and selectively reinforces change talk', responding to the client's feelings and issues so that initial resistance diminishes and the client's motivation and commitment to change is nurtured.

Phase 2 – Strengthening clients' commitment to change

The client's readiness to move into Phase 2 varies according to their internal motivational state. As mentioned, clients' entry states determine how quickly they can move into the second phase. Phase 2 processes involve the interviewer applying gentle pressure on the client, without confronting heavily which can further increase ambivalence or dissonance about change. The interviewer highlights the cost for the client of staying where they are and how current patterns are preventing goal achievement. This realization produces some level of dissonance. Many clients with addictive patterns of behaviour for example, are caught up in an approach-avoidance internal conflict. This may call for the amplification of discrepancies to help the client to formulate their own argument for change through seeing what their current behavioural patterns are costing them. This second phase also concerns helping clients to locate the right sort of action to achieve their outcomes. Processes of behaviour maintenance (and protecting the newly formed resolve) are part of this Phase. Miller and Rollnick (2002, pp. 128–129) suggest three hazards that can threaten the success of Phase 2, including 'underestimating clients' ambivalence' and both *over-prescribing* the plans and *providing insufficient direction* for these. In this respect they name common dilemmas for many interviewers in human service fields. Motivational interviewing, like the other approaches discussed in this chapter, has as its centre the view that clients, not the practitioner, make the changes. The emphasis is on building up a client's sense of optimism that change is possible, attainable and maintainable.

Miller and Rollnick's contribution is primarily in designing effective interview strategies that develop and maintain client motivation, enabling clients to forge a life without the damaging effects of self-defeating processes. They join other authors concerned with these internal cognitive-behavioural processes – for instance De Jong and Berg, (2008), Egan (2007) and McGuire (2000[a] and [b], 2004).

It is well accepted now that cognitive and behavioural processes can also be applied to a goal-focused and small step approach to change, to maintain clients' motivation and to instigate and support long-term change. This is an identified need for many clients and some principles of a cognitive-behavioural approach are described next, as these fit well with motivational work.

Key points about motivational approaches

➤ Without motivation clients lack any reason to take responsibility for changing things

➤ Clients vary in their level of motivation from pre-contemplation; contemplation; preparation; action or maintenance

➤ Stages in motivational work are building and strengthening clients' commitment to change

➤ Many clients are caught up in an approach-avoidance conflict on self-change

➤ Ambivalence undermines client commitment to change

➤ Avoid head-to-head confrontation of resistance and instead 'roll' with it

➤ Empathic responding is basic to the success of motivational approaches

➤ Client responsibility is a key feature of motivational approaches

➤ Motivational work is by its nature empathic, active and directive

Cognitive-behavioural strategies

In assisting clients to take better control over self-defeating thought and behaviour patterns many interviewers find the approaches applied in cognitive-behavioural therapy (CBT) can be effective in assisting clients in these areas. All applications of CBT of course need to be within a context of empathic work that has assisted the client to understand their situation, their feelings about it and how they are responding to life's pressures – perhaps in ways that are not functional. This level of understanding may take some time to develop – and may evade some clients all together. The application of CBT is most appropriate in later stages of work with clients, following adequate exploration of their issues supported through a strong and consistent empathic response structure.

Background issues in the development of CBT

Current cognitive-behavioural therapy (CBT) was developed as part of a wider battle over effectiveness in working with offenders and is featured in the 'What Works?' debate (Cameron and Telfer 2004, p. 47). Andrews and Bonta (2003 p. 437) say 'there is now a human science of criminal conduct' featuring 'how to make use of what works'. Several key aspects of offender intervention feature techniques and programs based around CBT (Cameron and Telfer 2004, p. 47 and Cameron 2006). It has a history too complex to do it justice in this chapter but McGuire (2000[b]) describes how the early theorists such as Mahoney (1974) and Meichenbaum (1977) adopted key principles including the role of the environment in learning. These ideas included key behavioural strategies, many of which are now well accepted in much mainstream interviewing work in a range of professions and settings. Several are suggested as key approaches in this book. For example, some of these focus on what we have discussed already – 'breaking complex behaviour into simple, more comprehensible units; the possibility of behaviour change in gradual, clearly defined steps; and the universal importance of monitoring and evaluation from outset to completion of the process, including follow-up to examine maintenance of change' and the use of 'self monitoring, self feedback and other self reports' (McGuire 2000[b], p. 20).

Continuing importance of inner language and self-talk in behaviour change

Many of these processes acknowledge the central importance of inner language or what I have referred to previously as *self-talk*, thus recognizing the 'central place of cognitive processes in self–regulation and self perception' (McGuire 2000[b], p. 20). These are well-known ideas now but this marriage between cognitive and behavioural approaches, formerly not well connected, produced what McGuire (2000[b], p. 20) terms 'powerful new approaches to understanding the complex dynamic relationships between thoughts, feelings and behaviour'. It seems odd that it took theorists and practitioners so long to understand that dependent, deviant and other dysfunctional behaviours in individuals are a product of cognition *and* behaviour, all surrounded by affect or feelings in their situations. Until these linkages occurred however, any consolidated or coherent set of approaches, effective in mediating a range of dysfunctional behaviours, remained elusive. According to Meichenbaum (1995), over this journey of discovery, cognitive-behavioural therapy had three principal stages and as McGuire (2000[b], p. 28) suggests these 'reflect wider developments in psychology itself' providing 'different metaphors for understanding the change processes in individuals'. These three stages were as follows:

Conditioning and cognitive learning theory

Learning theory is a basic premise of cognitive-behavioural approaches, with change conceptualized in terms of alterations in learning processes in the nervous system, involving thoughts, feelings and behaviours. As McGuire says (2004, p. 53), 'the conceptual framework of cognitive learning theory continues to evolve' but still provides the 'underpinning theoretical model' for most interventions comprising the CBT repertoire.

Cognitive information processing

The focus on cognitive events as prime factors influencing individuals and their difficulties took a strong hold in mental health work. More generally the key notions of cognitive therapies were spelt out by Ellis and Harper (1974) in their Activity–Behaviour–Consequences (ABC) analysis, as well as in Beck (1989) and others. This was followed by research according to McGuire (2000[b], p. 28) 'on how cognitive patterns support dysfunctional feelings and behaviour and on the nature and causes of these patterns themselves'. At least to some extent, consequences need to be seen as deriving from an individual's *management of own feeling reactions to events*. This intersects with clients' ability to separate feelings from behaviours. This, as I have discussed previously, is vitally related to the important principle of clients accepting responsibility for what they can take charge of – or in other words *self-control*. The intersection between behaviour, feelings and self-control is also noted by Andrews and Bonta (2003, pp. 127–128) for its application in working with offenders.

Self-attribution and constructive narrative

When it becomes clearer that behaviour is so closely related to feelings, thoughts and beliefs, or to cognitive events, ways to intervene in order to effect positive change in working with clients are better understood. How individuals construct these cognitive patterns – the internal narratives that emerge in the interviewing process (termed 'stories', by Ivey and Ivey 2003) – are all about how individuals create their own experiences. McGuire (2000[b], p. 29) describes this view of 'individuals as architects of their own individual existences' as a shift in the development of CBT, not yet fully resolved. I agree, as I think the process by which clients create their affective or emotional world and how this colours goal achievement in life is not yet fully accepted. For instance, many cling to the idea that feelings can be directly changed.

An important point to recognize in discussing CBT however is that there is no single cognitive-behavioural method or theory and that a variety of techniques and processes qualify for inclusion. McGuire (2000[b]) describes CBT as a *family* or collection of methods rather than a single technique although he does suggest (2000[b], p. 21) that self-instructional training (SIT) is seen as the 'core method of cognitive-behavioural therapy' or even 'the essence (sometimes even as the sum total) of the approach'. There are questions about whether CBT works for everyone and some question its applicability to females in correctional programs and to adolescents (Cameron and Telfer 2004; Cameron 2006). McGuire also suggests that some 'cognitive-behavioural approaches focus too heavily on internal, psychological events at the expense of external, environmental ones' (2000[b], p. 27).

There is a timely reminder here about the complex influences in clients' worlds which need to be considered in all stages of any rehabilitation or change process, and the importance of small behavioural steps towards change, within the capability of the client. So it is apparent that change-based approaches using CBT contribute strongly to a range of diverse methods that take into account the psychological, cognitive, behavioural, emotional and social needs of clients, within their usual environment. Many of the goal and action themes focused on in this book are cognitive-behavioural in origin. For example, my emphasis on helping clients to see the difference between feelings and behaviours, on self-talk, accepting responsibility for what they can change and on small baby steps toward client-defined solutions, are all CBT framed approaches and techniques.

Resilience in goal and action work

Resilience is a key concept in constructive change programs and of central interest when a cognitive-behavioural approach is used. Egan (2007, pp. 194–196) discusses two types of resilience which he attributes to the ideas of Holaday and McPhearson (1997) – *outcome* and *process* resilience. *Outcome* resilience is the ability of a person to 'bounce back' from a *one-off stressful or difficult life event* like loss of a job or a car accident. *Process* resilience refers to the kind of daily strength needed to keep managing a more constant difficulty, such as a chronic illness or constant stressful circumstances. A number of social and personal factors are believed to assist clients to weather life's challenges resiliently. These are described as a combination of 'social support, cognitive skills, and psychological resources' (Egan 2007, p. 194). *Social support* refers to the network of connections to people and organizations often referred to as *social capital* (Winter 2000), although the value of this might also depend on the characteristics of those to whom a person is connected. *Cognitive skills* to some extent derive from levels of intelligence and the ability to think through issues logically. These are also about cognitive style, such as self-talk or views of self-agency. *Psychological resources* may include a sense of humour, curiosity, flexibility and high energy as well as the ability to defer gratification in achieving long term goals. All of these social, cognitive and psychological skills forming the structure of a client's resilience are also part of the focus of many CBT approaches.

Solutions may remain evasive even when a small steps, CBT or motivational approaches are employed and attention is focused on supporting clients' self-esteem. Egan (2007, pp. 349–351) also refers to client inertia – where 'learned helplessness', 'disabling self-talk', 'vicious circles' and 'disorganization' may undermine the best of clients' plans. As well, entropy or 'the tendency of things to fall apart' (Egan 2007, pp. 351–352), means that even the most effective client work, can sometimes still break down. The resilient interviewer who is able to apply motivational, CBT approaches and small steps on the path towards change understands these tendencies and does not give up on clients who struggle to make productive changes in their lives.

Key points about Cognitive-Behavioural Therapy (CBT)

➤ CBT has its origins in the battle for effectiveness of offender-based programs, but is now accepted in mainstream interviewing work

➤ CBT theory comes from conditioning and cognitive learning theory, cognitive information processing and attribution and constructive narrative work

➤ CBT includes a broad family of techniques and strategies

➤ In this book, feeling and behaviour focused responding, utilizing the power of self-talk and formulating small goal steps towards change are all CBT techniques

➤ The construct of resilience is related to CBT, with focus on individuals' social support and psychological resources

CHAPTER OVERVIEW

This chapter has covered much ground in that it has reviewed client thinking patterns and managing client blind spots. Then several approaches related to goal identification and selection were described along with solution-focused action frameworks including motivational, cognitive-behavioural techniques and resilience factors in goal and action work. The next chapter focuses on some less usual aspects of client cases that add to the difficulty of clients' effecting positive change in their lives.

CHAPTER 7

Managing Crises: Violence, Self-Harm and Anger

In case the approach described at times in this book so far makes interviewing work seem unrealistically simple, this next chapter focuses on particular factors that may jeopardize successful interview outcomes. Client issues that cause stress to workers include crisis and especially suicide (statements, attempts and 'successes') and violence – to self and others (Corey and Corey 1999, p. 120). As well, premature termination of client–worker contact is stressful for workers. On this last point, there is some good news in that 78 per cent of single-session clients report feeling much better (Hutchins and Vaught 1997, p. 59), even if they do seem to terminate prematurely in terms of practitioner expectations. This chapter is devoted to perspectives on managing some of the harder edges of professional practice – the challenges involved in managing client crises including violence and self-harm issues and anger in the professional interview.

Crisis management in interviewing

Crises are very individually framed – and what pitches one person into a state of crisis may leave another just mildly disarrayed. Consequently, crises are not about events as such but rather a crisis in the interviewing context refers to the client's 'emotional reactions to a situation, *not* the situation itself' (Okun and Kantrowitz 2008, p. 252). The client's reactions to a range of external or internal events may immobilize their normal coping capacities. There is often a real sense of urgency and utter preoccupation with the situation or event. Many clients become overwhelmed by a range of feelings and discussion of suicide may set alarm bells ringing for many practitioners. In crises, including when suicide is considered, a sense of hopelessness and loss of self-esteem is often experienced, commonly combined with feelings of anxiety and fear. Okun and Kantrowitz (2008, p. 252) state that in a crisis a person may find 'that the ways they solved problems and coped with difficulties in the past no longer work' often causing them to lose faith in their own capacity to manage things and to become frightened for the future. When clients appear so helpless in the face of a crisis, practitioners may be tempted to offer advice straight away and to adopt a traditional counselling approach that focuses on the *problem* rather than applying a strength perspective. In crisis work however, as in any other aspect of interviewing, an empathic and focused approach is essential.

Sources of crises

Okun and Kantrowitz (2008) and Geldard (1998) discuss the range of origins and sources of crises in clients' lives. Understanding these when a client comes in for support and is obviously in a crisis state may be of use in deciding the kinds of support and care processes required to help the client to cope. Personal capacities and attributes of the client may be deeply implicated in their capacity to cope with events that others deal with much more easily. Some of these are referred to as 'dispositional crises' as in Okun and Kantrowitz (2008, p. 253) and are seen as reactions ensuing from the client being stretched beyond their usual information base and decision-making capacities. These might involve relatively simple things like choices about living arrangements or complex issues such as career changes.

Similar in a way are 'Anticipated life transitions' (Okun and Kantrowitz 2008, p. 253) or 'developmental crises' as described by Geldard (1998, pp. 193–194) in that these are common life events, often viewed as quite pleasant, that throw some people well off track – such as a promotion, marriage, or the birth of a child. Some of these so-called *normal* events are less positive and stretch everyone at least a little, such as a divorce or an illness, although for some clients these prove very stressful and precipitate a major crisis. Both Okun and Kantrowitz (2008, p. 231) and Geldard (1998, pp. 193, 194) mention that unresolved difficulties in negotiating normal developmental points in a client's life may re-appear in periods of stress. For example, relationship problems in adolescence may sit there as a kind of time bomb until an activating stressful event – like a relationship break-up in adulthood – results in a collapse that plunges the person back into the powerless feelings they experienced years before and into a current crisis.

Of course, some things can catapult just about anyone into a state of crisis including unexpected traumatic occurrences such as instances of rape, other assault, miscarriage of a pregnancy, sudden death of a loved one, a life-threatening illness, or a bad car accident, just to name a few. Most people's coping resources are severely stretched when things like this occur. Feelings of despair, anxiety and fear, depending on the severity of the event, are common. How quickly individuals recover from the trauma and get back to their usual level of coping may also depend on features of their personal control and resilience and developmental history, as well as on external supports.

It is the case that some people with less resilience and with personal tendencies to become highly anxious or depressed may suffer a 'psychopathological crisis' according to Okun and Kantrowitz (2008, p. 253). This occurs when any event mentioned so far, from everyday to traumatic, activates the individual's existing but normally better controlled neurotic tendencies. Where more serious psychiatric illnesses exist however, even if these are normally controlled through medication or other therapeutic processes, an episode of psychotic emergency may be activated by a challenging life event. This may result in reactions that pose possible dangers to self and others.

A crisis reaction in an individual is rarely able to be predicted, as this frequently results from a combination of personal, developmental and situational factors and for many clients the crisis is often about the proverbial straw that breaks the camel's back. De Jong and Berg (2008, p. 215) stress that it is always important to recognize the person's emotional reactions and their perceptions and cognitions about what has happened – as this can be quite idiosyncratic.

Interviewing emphases with clients in crisis

Compared with interviewing clients dealing with more 'normal' life issues, clients in a crisis situation often require some sharply focused strategies and approaches. For example, solution strategies focused on clients' *perceptions of immediate events* is encouraged along with promptly identifying the client's strengths in coping. Although noted as essential in crisis work, I believe this is important for most clients as there is little value in encouraging clients to drift onto issues from the past or future or to dwell on their problems without being helped to seek solutions that will work for them. In crisis work, it is essential to accurately assess the *sources* of stress and match these against an estimate of the client's coping capacities to manage them. Assisting clients to identify their pre-crisis functionality may assist in activating their normal resilience and strength in the face of this event. Existing client networks need to be identified as a resource and relevant people contacted to marshal additional practical and emotional support for the client. In the first instance, it may also be necessary to pay attention to reducing the client's stress through some brief relaxation therapy.

There is often a need for prompt practical and direct action with clients in crisis related to medical care, legal or burial arrangements, or emergency accommodation. Practical issues like these may need to be dealt with effectively before other psychological aspects can be addressed. Consequently, knowledge of effective referral resources is required to expedite this and the effective worker employs networks with agencies and services that offer resources and back-up support. Dependency of the client in crisis on the worker is common in the short term but Geldard (1998, p. 198) cautions against taking over for clients who may benefit from being supported in managing some practical arrangements themselves. In crisis situations where traumatic and serious events have occurred, it is also important to maintain a *reality* orientation by providing emotional support but no false reassurance.

What does managing a client in crisis mean in terms of the skills discussed so far? Responsive listening skills (empathy, affirming perceptions) are vital in dealing with clients in crisis. After the client is responded to, as they express feelings and thoughts, the process needs to move fairly quickly to coping strengths and solution building. Egan (2007, p. 225) suggests crisis intervention can be viewed as 'rapid application of the three stages of helping to the most distressing aspects' of clients' most urgent issues. It is important in the immediate term not to move onto other background life issues, as the client can rarely focus on anything except what is occurring in their life at that particular moment.

De Jong and Berg (2008, p. 220) suggest the use of 'coping questions' processes, rather than goal defining in crisis intervention. De Jong and Berg (2008, pp. 219, 220) warn that the 'miracle question' may not be very applicable in crisis situations, as clients often lack the capacity to think outside the frame at such times, although this needs to be tested with each client. In crisis counselling, solution-building processes are moved to promptly, so the strengths and capabilities of the client can be brought into play, setting up the feedback loop between positive self-esteem and coping actions. Following the immediate provision of appropriate emotional and practical support, De Jong and Berg (2008, p. 220) suggest it may be an opportunity to begin a process that enables the client to relocate their strengths and to manage their life again. Both Egan (2007) and De Jong and Berg (2008) stress worker empathy and the establishment of the 'working alliance' (Egan 2007, p. 49). It cannot be emphasized too strongly that clients in crisis situations cope best when they know their feelings and perceptions are understood, when a clear perception of their own strengths and abilities and available supports is established as early as possible and when the worker is well networked and competent.

When the situation has settled somewhat and the client is able to focus productively on their broader needs, then opportunities for counselling may be appropriate to enable their adaptation to the changed circumstances of their life. As Geldard (1998, p. 194) suggests, although crises are times of high risk or even danger for clients they may also be a 'time of opportunity'. A crisis may open a window into the client's life, shining light on other issues that bubbled up during the crisis period. For some clients then, it may be important after the urgent things have been managed to encourage them to see the immediate crisis as a prelude to further work, especially when the crisis reveals life issues needing attention. In some situations where grief and loss feature, it may be important to understand the distinct stages of the client's reaction to such events, as featured in the earlier work of Kubler-Ross (1970), and to work with them on ongoing grief management issues.

There are times however when nothing seems to offer any comfort or help to clients in extreme crises. Even De Jong and Berg (2008, pp. 232, 233), whose approach seems able to match the needs of most clients, admit there are points in working with clients in some crisis situations when everything seems too hard for clients go on coping. The client remains overwhelmed and does not seem to have either the inner or the outer resources to manage effectively. Referral to other sources of help or in some cases admission to short-term emergency care may become necessary. An interview characterized by empathic responding usually means the client is open to suggestions of calling on support from additional quarters. Clearly in such circumstances interviewers need accurate and up-to-date referral information, well-supported transfer procedures and the instigation of careful follow-up processes.

Key points about crisis management

➤ The sources of client crises and their capacities to cope with these are often developmental

➤ Events precipitating a crisis range from everyday occurrences to extremely traumatic ones

➤ Empathic responding to client perceptions about the crisis event is essential

➤ Immediate matters take precedence over more ongoing life management

➤ Stabilizing the client through stress management enables a focus on coping strengths

➤ The miracle question may have limited application in crisis management

➤ Offers of practical support need to fit around the client's capacity to manage aspects of this

➤ When coping capacities are absent, emergency care processes may be required

➤ Crises may uncover opportunities for further work on grief or life management issues

➤ Crisis work requires good referral sources with careful transfer and follow-up processes

Clients who threaten violence and self-harm

When a client presents with a crisis related to harming others or themselves, or these issues emerge after discussing other issues the practitioner is faced with some conflicting imperatives about protecting clients or others and juggling other professional obligations like confidentiality and duty to warn and/or report. Careful decision making, perhaps after seeking the support and guidance of supervisors or other wise counsel, is required and often there is limited time within which this can occur. Managing these different matters may make it difficult for practitioners to maintain competence, empathy and a clear head.

Violence may be part of clients' narratives – both as victims and as perpetrators. Women and children suffer more injuries deriving from violence, and many victims of abuse see themselves in a no-win situation. Perpetrators and victims have discrepant narratives about violence, so the issue is often difficult to resolve through talk in the practitioner's office (Wilmot and Hocker 2001, pp. 153–154). Causes of violence and abuse are mixed. These may be associated with overuse of alcohol and other drugs which have been consistently associated with violent and other anti-social behaviour in research spanning thirty years (Micsek 1994, pp. 381–493; Levinson 1994, pp. 15, 45; Scherwitz and Rugulies 1992, p. 81 and Shelden 2001, p. 187). But, the relationship between alcohol and violence to self and others is complex and socially imbedded because whilst it is accurate to say that over-ingestion of alcohol is associated socially with violence, 'there is controversy about whether the association is causative' (McDonald and Brown 1996, p. 20). Alcohol is apparently linked to loss of personal control, but why this leads to violence in some people and not others clearly depends on a range of other factors. It is apparent that alcohol's relationship with violence exists inside a complex set of determinants that are demographic, social and cultural, rather than just chemically based.

In terms of demography, younger people are especially vulnerable to all forms of violence – to self and others, especially between the ages of 18 and 30 (Carcach and Grant 2000) and for both perpetrators and victims according to the Australian Bureau of Statistics (1998). This is contrary to beliefs about older people being more at risk. Physical violence towards others is also associated with males, statistically five times more so than females (Mukjerjee et al. 1997). Self-harm is more prevalent among females (Mindframe 2006, p. 17). In Australia and in many other countries the most common kind of violence is 'confrontational violence between males, typically young and of marginal socio-economic status' (Hogg and Brown 1998, p. 53) and in Walker, Kershaw and Nicholas (2006, p. 75) in reference to the UK. The other most common violence is 'between family members and other intimates' (Hogg and Brown 1998, p. 53) as in domestic violence. So violence is likely to be part of many clients' lives and therefore features in many interviews in the human services.

McDonald and Brown (1996, p. 22) also demonstrate a coincidence between social disadvantage, violence and other anti-social acts across the Western world. Income inequality, low education levels, personal unemployment, family unemployment and poor housing are all linked to violence in the UK according to Walker, Kershaw and Nicholas (2006, p. 75). In Australia arrest rates for a range of crimes show indigenous males at around 30 per cent (ABS 1999), which could be linked back to gender (McDonald and Brown 1996, p. 25) but is more attributable to poverty than race. This pattern is reflected in most countries where first nation people are marginalized legally, socially and economically. Violence and child abuse have some consonance too and can occur in many families and other social settings regardless of social class or standing. Practitioners need to be alert to these issues emerging during clients' narratives.

Self-protective plans and clients with violent backgrounds

Helpers also need to have a self-protective plan when interviewing clients with violence patterns. Economic rationalism combined with deinstitutionalization of some mental health services has resulted in clients with serious mental health issues such as impulse control problems, being treated in community settings. This means at times that clients with at-risk patterns of behaviour including violent outbursts may not have been pre-screened and can turn up without any case notes to be seen by a lone female worker. Despenser (2007 online) identifies the risks faced by counsellors as including 'physical isolation, dangerous premises, some clients being seen without pre-screening, neglect of safety by counsellors and managers'. She also mentions that denial about risk by workers 'make it difficult for us to become conscious of threats and realistic limitations' (Despenser 2007). Also discussed by Despenser (2007) is the 'flawed logic' of making protective plans for meeting male clients in situations of some risk but not for females. Generally, it is suggested that in meeting all clients for the first time there is some protective plan in place and certainly so when the client has a known background of violence.

Clients who discuss suicide

Clients who express thoughts about suicide can cause many practitioners to be concerned and worried about their ability to prevent the client from acting on these thoughts. Corey, Corey and Callanan (2007, p. 590) note findings that list suicide statements by client as one of the most stressful client behaviours, followed closely by client anger and aggression towards the worker. Although there may be cases where it is not possible to prevent clients in the midst of deep despair from ending their lives, helpers feel a sense of failure when this does occur. One of my first clients, when I was a newly qualified psychological counsellor, took his own life after two appointments with me. His previous background of suicide attempts and mental illness absolved me from professional blame or responsibility by my colleagues but could not protect me from self-blame as I had felt quite unequipped to manage this person's needs.

Reeves and Nelson (2006 online) say 'it is impossible for counsellors to immunize themselves against the emotional demands experienced when working with suicidal clients, or the grief that is felt following a client suicide'. They underline the key importance of a 'good network of support' to prevent the impact of a client's death by suicide leading to what they term 'defensive practices' such as finding ways to avoid working with suicidal clients and justifying these reactions by referring to fear of litigation. De Jong and Berg (2008, p. 223) describe some defensive reactions of 'beginning practitioners' when clients discuss or *threaten* suicide in response to crises in their life. These include actively trying to talk clients out of their intentions and minimizing the client's level of serious intent, or on the other hand calling in the troops as it were – such as hospital staff or other medical support (De Jong and Berg 2008, p. 223) – so they can hand the problem onto someone else.

Is it possible to predict who will carry out their threats of suicide? Well not easily but some factors are worth considering as strongly indicating the seriousness of the person's threat. Corey et al. (2007, pp. 237–238) provide guidelines for assessing the risk of suicide in clients, although they too note it is not possible to either predict or prevent every suicide. In general if a client talks about suicide their intention needs to be taken very seriously – especially if they have a history of previous attempts, depression, sleep disruption and 'feelings of hopelessness and helplessness' (Corey et al. 2007, p. 237). Likewise a background of alcohol or drug abuse increases the risk of self-harm and suicide, as may other forms of psychiatric illness. Holmes and Holmes (2005, p. 136) state, 'There is no doubt that depression, alcohol and drugs are important indicators of a suicidal personality' although Corey et al. (2007, p. 238) also underline the significance of a good support base in preventing it.

Hutchins and Vaught (1997, p. 59) note the importance of particular procedures for dealing with violence or self-destructive behaviours in clients. Many of the processes recommended in dealing with crises in general can apply to working with clients who self-harm and/or appear to be at risk of suiciding. But many practitioners feel ill-equipped to manage such cases when the individual turns up or is brought along for an interview and their personal background is skimpy. De Jong and Berg (2008, p. 224) stress the essential value of using 'coping talk' with at risk clients. This is about recognizing that many clients who are deeply depressed, still do some things that are about *coping* – even in the midst of their despair. They may still be attending to other people's needs and if they have managed to get to the interview as well – this all needs affirming. Corey et al. (2007, p. 239) suggest that many clients benefit from being offered support to learn skills to apply to their immediate problems that may have seemed overwhelming to them before the suicide attempt.

Key points about violence and self harm issues

➤ Violence and self-harm, especially when suicide is discussed, present some of the most challenging matters

➤ Support and supervision are essential to help workers manage their feelings about suicide

➤ It is important to consider statistical indicators of violence and suicide

➤ A self-protective plan is considered essential with clients who have violent backgrounds

➤ Taking a solution-focused approach still applies with clients who discuss suicide

Professional obligations to warn and report

It is important to mention briefly here that practitioners need to address how to manage their professional mandate to report criminal behaviour – like child abuse, violence or other criminal matters – in the client's life. Mandatory reporting guidelines require most professionals, including psychologists, teachers, social workers and others, to report to the relevant authorities any reasonably well-founded suspicion that a client is involved as a victim or perpetrator of child abuse (Swain 2002, p. 33).

Likewise most practitioners will be required to warn relevant others of intentions to commit violent crimes, when the issue is one involving a serious threat to the safety of another person (Corey et al. 2007, pp. 224–256; Swain 2002, p. 34). Of course, national and/or state jurisdictions have different rules in this matter and all human service practitioners need to apprise themselves of these.

Especially sensitive collaboration early in the interview is sometimes required to explain the professional's mandated obligation to report suspected instances of child abuse, violence or other criminal matters. Corey et al. (2007, p. 224) refer to this range of obligations as 'the duty to warn and to protect'. They state this is about balancing clients' rights to privacy, confidentiality and free will with practitioners' responsibilities and obligations to protect the vulnerable and the community from violent behaviour and sometimes to save lives. This range of issues may become apparent at the beginning of the interview as the client's story unfolds, but may not surface until later as the client develops more trust in the practitioner. The requirements on reporting these matters run up against expectations about confidentiality between practitioners and clients. Crenshaw and Lichtenberg (1993, p. 183) suggest that professional reporting requirements generally override confidentiality guidelines in most human service work. McLaren (2007, p. 27) concludes that 'greater client knowledge on relationship boundaries may actually foster greater confidence in the worker, better help the development of a trusting relationship and provide opportunities for intervention where child abuse may exist'.

To manage any clash of expectations about confidentially then, clients need to be advised about the limits imposed by the interviewer's requirement to report or warn when protection issues surface. This occurs either at the beginning of an interview when it is known that child abuse or some other criminal matter is the focus of the discussion or whenever in the interview the client raises these issues. Managed well, this information need not discourage clients from continuing their narrative as, according to Swain (2002, p. 34), when professionals are appropriately open about this and suggest working through the implications for them and the client, trust need not be irreparably damaged. In fact, as Swain suggests, this honest and frank approach will be less damaging to trust than if a covert report is made later, about which the client is informed or finds out about in due course. Nonetheless, the estimation of the correct time to raise the issue is difficult for many practitioners and it is vital to manage the process carefully, courteously and honestly when it occurs.

There are other aspects of interviewing work where special skills and knowledge are required. This text moves on next to discuss working with anger, a set of processes requiring additional expertise in addition to those advocated so far.

Key points about obligations to warn and report

➤ Sensitive collaboration is required to explain professionals' mandated obligations

➤ It is essential to be familiar with national and/or state guidelines on mandatory reporting

➤ Requirements on warning and/or reporting can conflict with practitioner and client expectations about confidentiality

➤ An honest approach will be less damaging to trust than if covert actions follow

---

Managing anger in interviews

Managing anger with clients is an area which practitioners often see as quite challenging. In fact Corey et al. (2007, p. 590) rank it, after suicide talk, as second on the list of difficult moments for counsellors. Many people have difficulty with anger per se and when clients become angry, the discomfort of interviewers with their own and others' anger may cause their skills and effectiveness to fly out the window. Likewise some clients are also very uncomfortable with angry feelings and avoid their expression.

Practitioner and client anger

In particular, Corey and Corey (1999, pp. 91–93) discuss anger as a possible transference issue. Transference in clients means they are projecting onto the interviewer', feelings that someone else deserves such as their father or wife, for example. Displaced anger needs to be understood and carefully managed, but Corey and Corey (1999, p. 93) also suggest it is important to recognize that this is a two-way street. Workers' own transference issues may play a role, as can personal family injunctions and other unresolved experiences in dealing with own and clients' anger. This may mean that clients are on the receiving end of the helper's anger when they do not deserve it either. Anger may not just be a transference issue though, as many people – both client and counsellor – when they are stressed and overwhelmed by life's issues may 'lose it' and become unreasonably angry.

In reference to managing angry clients, it is also important to define professional limits – what is tolerable for the worker – and to set boundaries with clients who seem aggressively angry. This may also entail working out ways to deal with the anger of clients without rejecting them, which means managing the client's anger without personalizing it or becoming offended. Generally, in dealing with angry clients, interviewers should plan their escape from the interview room – and have a self-protective plan, as discussed previously. As well, it is essential for practitioners to reflect on their own feelings and to seek supportive supervision in managing clients who project a lot of anger. However, it is important to consider that sometimes a client's anger may be deserved – by the worker, and/or the agency. In such cases, it is essential to hear, acknowledge and accept it – and where possible to address the issue on behalf of the client.

Issues about expressed and repressed anger

Generally, the repression of anger is often considered bad for ones' health and well-being and it is thought better to 'let it all hang out'. Whether this is true or not is open to some debate. For some people, because there is discomfort with the direct expression of anger, passive-aggressive patterns that allow some of the repressed feelings to be expressed without owning up to them may become part of a person's style, as may the use of sarcasm. Free expression of anger can also be seen as socially unacceptable. Uncontrollable explosions of rage frighten not only the person on the receiving end, but also the 'expresser' at times. It is not uncommon for people to feel the need to apologize after the expression of strong, angry feelings, because it feels like some social or personal rule has been transgressed.

Stewart points out that most anger is *not* evidence of some deep psychological maladjustment or childhood trauma, rather it is simply one of our 'natural responses to things not going our way' (Stewart

1995, p. 417). Nonetheless, as Carr (1991, p. 111) suggests, individuals may become socialized out of openly expressing many feelings throughout childhood and adolescence. The social pressure to restrain one's anger increases as individuals move into adulthood. A poem by William Blake (1757–1827) entitled *A Poison Tree* (Erdman 1992) is often quoted to exemplify the damaging effects of being angry and keeping it bottled up.

> *I was angry with my friend: I told my wrath, my wrath did end.*
> *I was angry with my foe: I told it not, my wrath did grow.*

Not all agree however that it is always a good thing to express angry feelings. Beck notes some research indicating that expressing anger actually makes the person angrier (Beck 2000, p. 298). There is evidence that expressing anger can actually rehearse it and enhance the angry feelings. Beck (2000, p. 298) cites Tavris as suggesting that 'getting angry is cathartic only if you get a sense of control from the anger, whether this control is of own internal feelings or of the situation that was anger-provoking'. This might suggest that when a client seems to be working towards a state of high anger in their narrative it may not always be advisable to focus on and reflect angry feelings. In fact this may be counter-productive if it escalates their anger, as is suggested by Tavris and Beck (2000, p. 298), especially so if the client cannot differentiate between feelings and action, as discussed previously.

Anger, stress and hostility

Related to Tavris' point (in Beck 2000, p. 298) there are other interesting findings coming from research, suggesting that stress, anger, hostility and aggression all sit together in a person's communication profile. Swan (1998) suggests that whenever people have increased levels of anger and hostility, their stress and the health-damaging effect of it increase as well. Anger, stress and aggression all appear to have a range of social and health effects, including higher incidence of cancer, depression and heart attack. It is not good for individuals to be hostile. It is clear that those people who are more predisposed to react to other people and to life events generally with increased anger and hostility could be shortening their life span. A complex set of psycho-social variables are involved with individuals with high levels of hostility, but these can be difficult to unravel. It is true that anger itself cannot damage another person and it is essential to distinguish it from aggression. Johnson (1997, p. 298) notes the down side to anger when it is aggressively expressed, such as its intimidating impact on others and the door it may open towards physical aggression and violence in some people.

For some clients there is little doubt that anger is the emotional impetus of their physically aggressive outbursts, leading on occasions to violence toward friends and family members – as discussed previously. For such clients, anger management skills may need to be the primary focus of the interview. Behaving aggressively or even violently towards family members may lead to feelings of regret when the storm has passed. For this reason, when the issue and the relationship are both important to clients, understanding how they can express anger non-aggressively rather than reacting impulsively and violently may become the focus of the intervention.

This range of issues become more complex when the interviewer has a *duty of care* over members of a family where the client's anger and related aggression is a self-control issue connected to domestic violence. The interview may need to focus on clients' understanding of the difference between feelings and behaviours and taking responsibility for own behaviour, as has been discussed previously. Some clients have complex needs in this area and there is much more to be understood in this area of anger management with clients involved in domestic violence. This is an important area requiring much greater detail than is possible within the scope of this book and Berkowitz (2000) is recommended as further reading.

The uses of anger

Anger is not always bad news. Johnson (1997, pp. 298–299) also points out that anger can be a useful emotion in that it can push people towards solution-seeking actions. Johnson suggests anger can give people energy, provide strength to protest against the wrong actions of others and inspire individuals to be braver in the face of injustice for instance. However, most people remain uneasy about expressing anger and clients may need help in managing this volatile aspect of emotional expression. Remaining calm in the face of own or another's anger is difficult. Own anger requires good concentration and self-control, as anger can be rather righteously self-absorbing (Johnson 1997, p. 247).

Key points about anger management

➤ Issues about the repression or expression of anger are important

➤ Anger is cathartic only if a sense of control is gained from its expression

➤ Anger, hostility and stress may be health damaging

➤ Anger is a feeling but its uncontrolled expression may result in physical aggression and violence

➤ Anger management may be a key feature of interviewing work with some clients and duty of care issues may relate to domestic violence

➤ Anger has use in energizing and motivating individuals to move against injustices

CHAPTER OVERVIEW

In this chapter, the complexities of dealing with a range of crisis-based issues including issues related to violence and self-harm including suicide were discussed. These issues clearly invoke the practitioner's duty to warn and protect clients and this was linked at times to matters of self-protection. Discussed also was the expression of anger in the interview setting. The chapter has suggested the ongoing value of the empathic enterprise but advocates a range of additional processes when situations demand it.

The next chapter moves on to explore the value of effective stress management related to the pressures and stress of professional interviewing discussed in previous chapters and avoiding professional burnout. The importance of a reflexive approach to practice is suggested as a self-protective set of strategies with life-long applicability.

CHAPTER 8

Self-care in Counselling

All of the preceding challenges alone might suggest the task of inter-viewing especially in human services settings is riddled with stress for the practitioner. Certainly, there are indications that practitioners need to look after their own health and well-being and manage stress and pressure in their work, so this is the focus of the final chapter. The ability to recognize and deal with stress is coupled with an ability to maintain a reflexive approach to professional learning and life.

Stress, burnout and surviving these is a major theme in the first section of this chapter. Modern life is redolent with stress for many individuals. The pace of life seems faster and the weight of expectations about success seems unrelenting for many. People seek solace in drugs and other dis-tractions that may deplete their reserves of energy, making them more vulnerable to the further impact of stressors on their system.

Defining stress

Stress is defined by most theorists as the individual's reactions to stres-sors – rather than the actual stress-producing occurrence itself. This is because individuals' reactions to known stressful events are so idiosyn-cratic that these offer no benchmark in defining what an individual finds stressful. What one person finds mildly irritating, another will experience as unbearably stressful. So Beck (2000, p. 270) rejects a simple *stimulus* definition of stress and any response-based definition. He favours a more *interactive* framework that combines the *situational stimulus variables* (trauma, life changes, hassles) with those of the *person's perceptions about their capability to cope with this stimulus* (susceptibility, personal control, attribution, self-talk and lev-els of self-esteem).

At a very basic level, reactions to situations of stress are based in human survival instincts – the old 'flight or fight' response mechanism, where 'your body prepares itself, when confronted by a threat to either stand ground and fight or run away' (Greenberg 1996, p. 4). Reactions to events and occurrences involve a mixture of biological, physiological, social and/or philosophical factors of the individual. Seyle found in his research that 'regardless of the sources of the stress, the body reacted in the same way' (in Greenberg 1996, p. 4). Beck (2000, p. 269) describes what he terms the 'general adaptation syndrome' or GAS, also based on Seyle's earlier work.

Three phases of the general adaptation system (GAS)

Alarm or reaction

Alert! Alert! Tiger in the camp! In this first stage the body releases adrenaline and sets in place a range of psychological and physiological changes to prepare the individual to deal with the threat. This is the old fight or flight response described by Greenberg (1996) and Beck (2000). Adrenalin is circulated. The heart beats faster sending more blood around the muscles and other body systems in preparation for sudden movement (running away or fighting with the tiger!). Breathing increases (more oxygen is needed for the hard-working heart and muscles), pupils dilate (increasing night vision and general visual acuity), the stomach and intestines may void with diarrhoea or vomiting occurring, or at least the person may feel like doing so. This is about lightening the body in preparation for easier fleeing or fighting. These reactions happen quite suddenly in the case of a severe perceived threat. Once the immediate danger (e.g. the tiger) is removed, the body gears down to a less extreme state.

Resistance or adaptation

Stay fairly alert in case the tiger comes back! If the cause for the stress reaction continues then the general adaptation system or GAS goes to the next stage of *resistance or adaptation*. The person remains in a state of anxiety but adapts to this. The level of system reaction is not as extreme as in the previous stage as this would be unsustainable for the body. Different hormones are circulated to increase blood sugar levels to sustain energy and some higher levels of adrenalin continue, keeping up blood pressure. Other sustainable changes occur such as increased production of corticosteroids to maintain strength, endurance and immunity in the short term. If this continues without a chance to get away from real or imagined danger and this state of sustainable readiness is maintained, things start to go seriously wrong. The person may have trouble sleeping or concentrating. They become tired and/or irritable and maybe depressed. They may also feel angry, become aggressive (or try to restrain these unsociable aggressive impulses). Individuals may also try to avoid it all – either physically and/or psychologically, naturally or chemically.

Exhaustion

We know the tiger might still be out there but there is nothing to be done about it and we just have to cope with our anxiety and get on with food gathering, hunting and looking after our families. This is the final GAS stage and results from the resistance/adaptation changes rolling through the person's system. Now, however, the body begins to run out of its reserves of energy and immunity. Mental, physical and emotional exhaustion begins to develop and as a result there may be decreased stress tolerance. The tiger is still there (at least in the mind) but now the person has few reserves left to deal with it all and still has to cope with life's continuing demands. Of course there are no tigers in modern society and situations are usually not so extreme, although other threats loom large and nibble at the edges of the mind.

A case study of stress

Joan is a social worker by background but now has a high-powered position managing a large human service organization. She likes her job although she finds it stressful at times. It often requires her to put in very long hours and to work on weekends. She has not taken a holiday for nearly two years. She has a tendency to become very tense when there are work pressures, such as report deadlines. She has mild anxiety symptoms for which she was medically treated in the past year.

Recently she has been involved in an organizational downsizing activity where she oversaw the firing of a number of older workers and the hiring of a few younger and better qualified ones. This made her very unpopular with the rank and file of her organization. Yesterday she came home from work to find a threatening piece of mail calling her a tyrant and besmirching her character. She links this to several phone calls – hang-ups – she received at home in the last week. She notified the police and they have promised to keep a watch on her house. She is a single parent of a daughter (16) and she now fears for her safety too. She does not know where to turn for support on this issue which has badly shaken her. She has no relatives close by on whom she can rely. Her only friends are in her work setting and she does not feel comfortable telling them what is happening.

This is how Joan's stress reactions may unfold
Alarm reactions occur – with high emotional arousal, anxiety and worry about her own safety and that of her daughter. She also feels guilty about being a working mother and bringing this trouble into her home. Her system remains on high alert. She feels very uptight, has trouble getting to sleep and when she does she wakes several times, alert to every little noise. During the night she turns the situation over and over in her head. She feels very worried that her distress is impacting on her job. During the next day she has a headache, diarrhoea and cannot eat much. She runs a disaster-focused line of self-talk in her mind and keeps picturing worst case scenarios involving her dismissal, masked men in the night and letter bombs being found and opened by her daughter.

Resistance or adaptation begins. Joan's system stays in a state of arousal but she needs to push down these feeling to keep coping with her job. She finds it hard to concentrate on work issues, makes several bad mistakes and notices others at work seem to be looking at her strangely. Joan is forced to take a couple of days off sick but while away from work she worries about what is happening and fears about losing her job rise up. She starts drinking quite a bit at night and takes sleeping pills in an effort to get to sleep and to blot it all out. She tells herself she has to cope better than this but is beginning to fear where it will all end.

Exhaustion from repeated alert/resistance processes leads to deeper psycho-physiological changes in Joan's body. The ongoing stress produces some cardiovascular changes as her heart struggles under constant high anxiety. She develops symptoms of angina. As well, gastrointestinal changes occur from the ongoing diarrhoea, drinking and poor diet – and a duodenal ulcer begins to develop. Finally immunological changes happen as her system becomes run down from lack of sleep and poor nutrition and she catches a bad cold which she cannot seem to get over. As Joan's exhaustion, illness and lack of support continue she becomes depressed and feels she just cannot face work. Her doctor has put her on a range of medication for her physical ailments and now he prescribes a course of anti-depressives. Joan applies for a period of protracted sick leave. She has a sinking feeling about ever facing work again.

Susceptibility and resistance to stress

Understanding susceptibility uncovers what may also be protective factors in reference to the damaging impact of stress. Individuals vary in how they handle stressful events and some people seem able to process stress better than others – that is they do not seem to lose their coping capacity and manage to keep on top of things.

Beck (2000, pp. 274–275) discusses a survey of a range of research on predictors of individual stress resistance and its management. Some of the factors related to resistance may be *genetic* in nature and Beck points out how temperament and stress resistance is bred into or out of dogs as examples. As well, very early experience both *prenatal* and *postnatal* (Beck 2000, p. 274) is well understood as indelibly influencing personality type including stress reaction patterns. Trauma in *childhood* from a range of events related to parenting style and other issues may be significant in stress resistance. Treatment by peers *in adolescence* also influences a person's confidence and impacts on self-esteem. These experiences feed into an individual's self-talk and ultimately into stress resistance and management patterns – with experiences and thought patterns forming a *self-sustaining loop*. So by the time a person reaches adulthood they may have stress reaction patterns almost hard-wired into their response repertoire. Where these are negative in nature, on a more positive note, re-decisions can be taken during life, meaning that some individuals are able to improve their stress management patterns. Although according to Beck (2000, p. 283) there may be a strongly genetic quality in personality factors, fortunately for most people coping well with stress is also a matter of adaptation or learning. A solution-focused approach to life (as has been discussed in this book generally) and the use of stress management techniques, as discussed later in this chapter, can ameliorate the negative impact of life's stressors.

Control issues and stress

Beck (2000, pp. 282–287) also notes a number of factors that appear to protect the individual from the damaging effects of stress. Certain personality features assist in coping with stress. The individual with what is termed a 'hardy personality is said to be committed to goals rather than alienated from life, to treat life's frustrations as challenges rather than threats and to feel in control of his or her own life' (Beck 2000, p. 282). As well extraversion and optimism relate to a person being 'open, talkative, adventurous and sociable' and 'happier and more optimistic' as well as 'less prone to stress problems' (Beck 2000, p. 283).

Central in a person's reaction to environmental stress is the issue of perceived control over life events (Beck 2000, pp. 275–281) and this may be *predictive, illusory, vicarious* or *interpretive* control. *Predictive* control allows failures to be minimized (So what – I knew this was going to happen); *illusory* control is where a chance happening is attributed to skill (I can control the dice); *vicarious* control is about handing over decisions to a higher power (God will protect me) and *interpretive* control is about the person finding meaning in life's uncontrollable happenings ('This was meant to happen to teach me something'). Perceptions about personal control colour a person's ability to manage the stress factors in their life and intersect with issues around negative self-talk, learned helplessness and locus of control.

The issue of locus of control has been discussed previously in reference to clients' abilities to cope and to levels of resilience. In stress management, those individuals who are best able to manage are likely to have a sense of their own power or capabilities rather than feeling helpless in the face of stressors. Beck (2000, p. 280) discusses the work of Seligman who saw learned helplessness was related to depression and a generally hopeless perspective on the world. Those with an internal locus of control also do not usually feel helpless – and these two concepts seem to be related.

It is important, however, to differentiate between personal qualities and strategies that help a person to function effectively despite stress in their life, and other approaches characterized by *denial* of the damaging impact of highly stressful events. For example, even though an event is highly traumatic – such as an accident or a personal attack – the person may appear to be coping with it in the short term because they are in denial about it. As the weeks unfold, however, it may become apparent that although outwardly calm or cheerful at deeper levels the stress has been eating away at the person. Weeks or even months later they may begin having flashbacks to the traumatic event, have trouble sleeping, become anxious or depressed and lose their capacity to cope. This is termed Post-Traumatic Stress Disorder or PTSD (Beck 2000, p. 270). This human tendency – to carry on coping in the face of trauma, life changes, heavy workload and frustrating conditions – may also be related to the phenomenon of a more gradual disintegration of the practitioner's equilibrium, termed professional burnout.

Professional burnout

Whitehead, Ryba and O'Driscoll (2000, p. 52) state that 'Freudenberger (1974) and Maslach (1976) coined the term burnout to describe a particular kind of stress response experienced by those working in the helping professions, such as nurses, social workers, police officers and educators'. Generally it is a feature of work linked with *emotional labour* rather than physical work. Buys and Kendall (1998, p. 2) define burnout as physical and emotional exhaustion that is specifically related to the workplace. Pines, Ben-Ari, Utasi and Larson (2002, p. 257) refer to burnout as 'state of physical, emotional and mental exhaustion caused by long-term involvement in situations that are emotionally demanding'. Bride, Robinson and Figley (2003, p. 1) also refer to this sort of stress as being due to 'indirect exposure to traumatic events' that are experienced by clients and James and Gilliland (2001, p. 666) relate it to professionals internalizing their clients' trauma. Kottler (2000, pp. 76, 84) suggests that all these ideas help to acknowledge that involvement with clients who have experienced pain and distress draws deeply on the personal reserves of practitioners.

As in stress generally, professional burnout usually has early warning signs although these may be quite idiosyncratic depending on the individual practitioner's general resilience and the organizational nature of their work. Jackson and Donovan (1999, p. 113) note the importance of differentiating between personal and organizational sources of burnout and that the term 'job burnout' is used 'when the cause lies in the workplace'. However, they admit it can be difficult sometimes to make this distinction. Buys and Kendall (1998, p. 3) note that a study of newly qualified human service workers showed that 'burnout was associated with two multidimensional factors, namely the qualities of the individual worker and the demands of the organisational environment'. This is logical as it is clear that environmental work factors can impact on the practitioners' skills and qualities in managing stress, just as individual stress management and other lifestyle issues can have 'organisational consequences' (Jackson and Donovan 1999, p. 113). Whitehead et al. (2000, p. 53) state that 'emotional exhaustion, a core component of burnout, is characterized by fatigue and weariness that develop as emotional energies are drained'. Cooper (1995) suggests the link to a range of factors, including genetic predisposition, environment, experience, business type and management and lifestyle choices.

Symptoms of professional burnout

A diagnosis of professional burnout can be made on the basis of three main symptoms according to Cooper (1995, online). These include *detachment* (especially from clients and staff); *exhaustion* (physical and especially emotional) and *loss of satisfaction* with a limited sense of accomplishment. The only signs for some may be chronic fatigue to the point of exhaustion, extreme tiredness and a sense of being physically run down. These symptoms may be accompanied with cynicism, negativity, suspiciousness, feelings of helplessness and irritability.

All counsellors may sometimes have a sense of being besieged, which can lead to episodes of angry outbursts at seemingly inconsequential things. Greenberg (1996, pp. 257–258) notes a range of indicators that burnout may be relatively imminent. Some of these include accepting overtime, putting off vacations, missing lunch and skipping breaks; increased physical symptoms such as aches and pains and fatigue; social withdrawal from usual friends, workmates and family; psychological changes similar to those mentioned by Cooper (1990) such as 'diminished sense of humour', depression, loss of self-esteem, pessimism, paranoia and difficulty making decisions (Greenberg 1996).

Many of these changes may be exacerbated by the professional self-medicating on alcohol or other prescribed and un-prescribed drugs. Cooper (1995) notes the link between high stress and loss of self-control in one's life. Anger at those making demands or alternately self-criticism for putting up with such demands may result. A range of physical symptoms are noted as being associated with burnout as for other forms of stress, such as frequent headaches and gastrointestinal disturbances, weight loss or gain, sleeplessness and shortness of breath. There may also be increased degrees of risk taking – as in abuse of alcohol, illegal drugs, gambling and unsafe sex (Cooper 1995).

Learning to survive – strategies to manage stress and burnout

Stress is inevitable in most professional work and seems more likely when work is emotional in nature and involves a heightened sense of obligation towards one's clients as is common in the human services. Stress control becomes a feature of survival as this is about preparing individuals for the realities of the workplace as well as using stress management practices after encountering stressful work situations. More detailed stress control strategies than are possible to list in this section are usefully incorporated in both entry-level and in-service education for professional practice. This would provide some protection against the risks of burnout. However, there are also some important organizational processes requiring attention, as indicated by Maslach and Leiter (1999), where managers and others need to encourage and support healthy work practices.

Organizationally located strategies

The research of Maslach and Leiter (1999) identifies six key areas for focus in avoiding or dealing with symptoms of burnout. They suggest the following need to be established: 'a manageable workload, a sense of control, the opportunity for rewards, a feeling of community, faith in the fairness of the workplace and shared values' (Maslach and Leiter 1999, p. 51). It is significant that traditional individual stress management processes, such as relaxation classes or stress counselling, are not especially emphasized here although they certainly suggest taking responsibility for making changes by getting involved, taking the initiative, breaking the issue down into manageable tasks and suggesting a problem solving approach (Maslach and Leiter 1999, p. 53). An organizational approach is also reflected by Buys and Kendall (1998) who, while accepting that there is some role for individualized processes in minimizing stress and burnout, conclude there are usually 'human resource management and educational implications that must be addressed' (Buys and Kendall 1998, p. 12).

For stress that is not just about the workplace, though it may be part of it, there are obvious issues of personal management and different strategies that relate to them, linking with those identified by Maslach and Leiter (1999) but stretching more widely. Dealing with life's stress is an ongoing process and strategies for managing stressful settings are important. These include looking after self and protecting personal space, peace of mind, self-esteem and sense of own competence. This may mean avoiding some people's company or not attending a particular event or meeting.

Maintaining physical health and well-being

Maintaining one's equilibrium despite needing to deal with stressful situations and difficult people is also about using strategies to support personal strength and resilience both mentally and physically. Gorkin (2005, online) says that regular physical exercise 'releases the body's natural pain killers and mood enhancers' which he says are 'important, in times of stressful transition'. Other processes that maintain health and well-being in the face of stressful circumstances are eating healthily, finding diverse ways to relax and visiting quiet calm settings before or after encountering stressful situations. It may also be helpful to seek the company of people who are supportive both before, for an injection of positive affirmation, and after a stressful episode for a chance to debrief.

Defending oneself with communication skills

Some stressful situations need to be faced and managed, as they are part and parcel of one's job. The emphasis here is on developing social and emotional skills that help one cope with stressful events that cannot be avoided. Learning to be assertive and developing skill in managing conflict and other effective communication skills are all useful strategies. Generally stress is less when one has supportive interpersonal relationships and this may mean using communication to develop networks and to better value and grow relationships, thus increasing the amount of support one can call on.

Building internal control

This area is focused on internal processes that build a greater sense of control over own feelings and reactions within situations and over one's internal dialogue so as to build better self-esteem and confidence. Likewise effective time management skills may be part of personal control and assist in limiting pressure in some settings. Developing a more internal framework and emphasizing responsibility for one's outcomes also known as self-efficacy (Bandura 1989, in Myers 1993, p. 107) may be part of gaining better control as discussed in Chapter 6. Internal control work may also entail focusing on mind and body connections and internal dialogue issues to bring down levels of tension and anxiety.

Growing resilience in self and others

It was noted in Chapter 6 that resilience in clients appears to comprise a combination of 'social support, cognitive skills, and psychological resources' (Egan 2007, p. 195 citing Holaday and McPherson 1997). A concept related to resilience is that of 'hardiness' as discussed by Greenberg (1996, pp. 126–128) and which he relates to a person's levels of *commitment, control* and *challenge*. Commitment refers to how willing a person is to get involved or to engage with people and events. Control is a concept discussed previously and it relates to self-efficacy and is directly linked to belief in own ability to influence outcomes. Challenge is a mind-set phenomenon where a person believes that change and stress are normal parts of life and may present opportunities for personal growth.

Gorkin (2005, online) states that that 'during the break up of Ma Bell in the '80s, researchers discovered four factors that distinguished' those who became victims of extreme stress from those who survived or even thrived. Based on what was found, Gorkin identifies four key aspects of 'psychological hardiness'. Two of these – 'commitment' and 'control' – seem very similar to those identified by Greenberg (1996). The third factor which he terms 'change' is similar to Greenberg's 'challenge' as Gorkin describes this as follows: 'Hardy players viewed change as a stepping stone not a stumbling block'. Gorkin calls his fourth quality 'conditioning' and this is about 'regular physical exercise' which he says is important in times of extreme stress. 'Exercise grounds us when everything else seems up in the air' (Gorkin 2005).

Support and supervision as stress management

Generating protective qualities in the face of stressful work circumstances may not be easy sometimes. The practitioner needs to put in place ongoing strategies to protect psychological health as a *preventative* process rather than implementing emergency measures after the work situation has escalated to one of high stress. It is noted by Krahn, Thom, Hale and Williams (1995) that there is value in learning to recognize at-risk patterns in the work setting and to consider how styles of management may predispose practitioners to high levels of stress and burnout. Seeking preventive support from supervisors in managing physical, emotional and cognitive problems may be a chance for practitioners to learn more about stress management, to take greater control over their work and personal life, to develop personal strategies and perhaps even to influence the organization to respond more constructively to the problem of staff stress and burnout.

It is apparent from the preceding discussion that managing stress and avoiding professional burnout involves a set of interconnected skills and processes. These focus on networks of connections to people and organizations (or social capital); cognitive skills in managing positive self-talk; psychological skills including humour, curiosity and flexibility; maintaining fitness and energy through exercise and seeking good support. All of these features are part of the individual's resilience and hardiness and are worth considering in focusing on own stress management skills and those of clients.

Bernstein (1999, pp. 137–163) recognizes the complex range of pressures present in much professional work and suggests the importance of several key processes in managing these. In terms of individualized strategies, she too mentions time management and cognitive, physical and emotional self-care. In reference to organizational aspects she notes the importance of supervisory support, especially when difficult situations arise for which workers may not have the personal resources to manage.

Current work in many fields in the human services presents interviewers with a range of challenges and pressures but overall there is the chance to make a positive difference – to impact on clients' lives for the better. Sustainable interviewing in the human services takes place inside a framework that includes self-care, reflective self-awareness and the ability to respond with deliberate and empathic effectiveness. In acknowledgement of the pressures of interviewing, this chapter now concludes with a focus on the importance of maintaining reflexive approaches to practice and ongoing learning in one's profession.

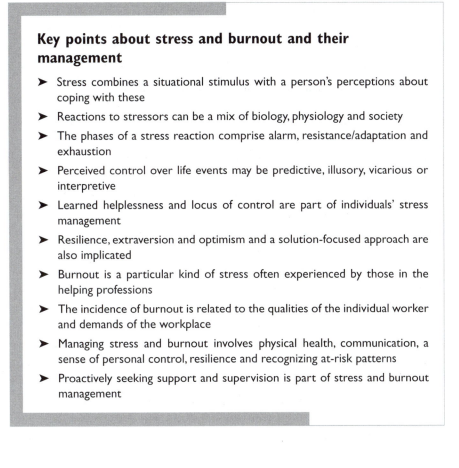

Key points about stress and burnout and their management

➤ Stress combines a situational stimulus with a person's perceptions about coping with these

➤ Reactions to stressors can be a mix of biology, physiology and society

➤ The phases of a stress reaction comprise alarm, resistance/adaptation and exhaustion

➤ Perceived control over life events may be predictive, illusory, vicarious or interpretive

➤ Learned helplessness and locus of control are part of individuals' stress management

➤ Resilience, extraversion and optimism and a solution-focused approach are also implicated

➤ Burnout is a particular kind of stress often experienced by those in the helping professions

➤ The incidence of burnout is related to the qualities of the individual worker and demands of the workplace

➤ Managing stress and burnout involves physical health, communication, a sense of personal control, resilience and recognizing at-risk patterns

➤ Proactively seeking support and supervision is part of stress and burnout management

The value of reflexive learning in practice

To maintain equanimity in the face of the range of challenges both external and internal discussed throughout this book practitioners in all areas of work in the community need to use reflective and reflexive processes. The final area discussed in this book is the development of the habit of self-appraisal, reflection and reflexivity to deal with the challenges of work in the field. This is about becoming a reflexive lifelong learner.

Layers of learning in reflexive practice

In explaining reflexive learning, Taylor and White (2000, p. 198) begin by defining two layers of reflection. The first layer of reflection concerns 'the process of thinking about our practice at the time (reflection-in-action)', which is the sort of 'thinking on your feet' experienced most by practitioners. They suggest this needs to be followed with a deeper layer of reflection 'after the event' which they refer to as 'reflection-on-action'. Reflexivity includes these two separate reflective processes, but pushes further (or bends back) to interrogate the basic premises of knowledge (Cameron 2003, p. 369) questioning the 'taken-for-granted assumptions' (Taylor and White 2000, p. 198) or the 'tacit' nature of theory (Schön 1991, p. 255).

The ongoing development of the reflexive worker is a matter of deep interest to some who see that essential layers of learning flow from the experience of reflective practice. Fook (in Pease and Fook 1999) also considers self-appraisal and reflection an essential aspect of practice, as do Taylor and White (2000). Barnett (1997, pp. 163, 164) suggests moving beyond self-reflection in learning to what he terms the critical (or reflexive) level of being. He suggests this requires a 'three-pronged approach' incorporating 'critical reason, critical self-reflection and critical action' – or the interplay of 'knowledge, self and the world' (Barnett 1997, p. 8). This is a reflexive level of contemplation. Such a perspective demands that practitioners review the knowledge acquired in their professional education and re-examine this in terms of their current milieu of practice with the whole process feeding into a deeper process of 'critical self-reflection' as described by Barnett (1997, p. 8). Theory, skills and values, learned during professional education, are re-examined with a critically reflexive eye (Cameron, 2003, p. 369) and deeply questioned in terms of their relevance for current practice.

Taylor and White (2000, p. 198) suggest that more than incident-focused reflection is needed if professionals are to avoid taking knowledge and skills as well as agency practice for granted. To the reflexive learner or practitioner, all knowledge is open to scrutiny and is able to have its most basic foundations questioned for relevance or even accuracy. However, reaching this viewpoint is made more possible when pre-practice learning is reflexive, so students acquire the habit of interrogating knowledge as they accrue it during study and then take this into their working lives.

Matthews and Candy (1999, p. 50) suggest that most work knowledge occurs 'incidentally or adventitiously' so that effective practitioners favour what is termed 'generative or anticipatory' learning in the workplace, rather than 'reactive or maintenance' learning. This requires a reflexive stance – both to recognize new knowledge and to avoid the blinkered vision that comes from blind acceptance of previous theory and ideas (Cameron 2003, p. 370). Edwards, Ransom and Strain (2002, p. 533) suggest that reflexivity leads to 'a growing understanding of customary practice' and to the 'transformation of habitat'. For practitioners in many professional areas, this means challenging institutional policy and practices and maybe at times 'to convert situationally specific, informal hunches into well framed theories of practice' (Brookfield 1992, p. 80) or new knowledge. However, challenging standing practices and building new ways of knowing requires well-established reflexive processes, to provide ballast against organizational opposition to change and institutional and personal dogmatism (Cameron 2003, p. 370).

Challenges to the reflexive mode of practice

As found by Cameron (2003, p. 370) and reported also in Taylor and White (2000), several other features of practitioners' experiences push up against reflexive practice and endanger the chance for practitioners to become 'critical beings', to use Barnett's term (1997). Both opportunities for and challenges to reflexivity occur when new practitioners discover the actual work is different in reality, compared with that described in their professional education. O'Connor et al. (1998, p. 3) suggest that practitioners 'find it hard to reconcile the image of the highly trained professional with the apparently mundane activities undertaken in their day-to-day work'. For practitioners able to use a reflexive approach, this point of realization is an opportunity for new knowledge building; for others it marks a movement into anger and personal and professional cynicism and the danger of burnout.

Schön (1991, p. 11) too notes the 'gap between the school's prevailing knowledge and the actual competencies required of practitioners in the field'. As Taylor and White (2000, p. 199) suggest, all that knowledge must be understood and then critiqued as fixed pieces of information about the world, made by (academic) others. Taylor and White (2000, p. 200) stress that 'unexamined forms of realism, whether objectivist or subjectivist, are problematic foundations on which to build professional practice'. They elevate the processes of reflexivity to its role of knowledge making – the processes involved in understanding 'how practitioners make knowledge in their daily work routines' (Taylor and White 2000, p. 201). This is similar to the 'situated learning' discussed by Usher, Bryant and Johnston (1997, pp. 169, 170) who note that this 'situatedness' itself requires reflective critiquing as a key aspect. They suggest that a view of action broader than the work setting is required – what they term 'reflection–outside action' (Usher et al. 1997, p. 170) to avoid the silo effect of a mainstream practice orientation. This suggests that practitioners may need to have coaches or mentors who are not part of their work settings and who are beyond the mainstream views of their professions. O'Connor et al. (1998, pp. 229–230) describe 'self-reflexive practice' as essential for practitioners to negotiate the moral frames underlying practice. They caution against practitioners being blind to implicit flaws in learned practice knowledge, indicating the need for wider views, or 'thinking outside the professional square' again (Cameron 2003, p. 372).

However, Parsloe (2001, p. 11) says that 'what happens between action and reflection' is a grey territory. But she is certain, as am I, that competent practitioners in a range of professional settings 'have to have the confidence to act in often very difficult circumstances but at the same time to hold open the possibilities that they may be wrong or that there is a better way they could be acting' (Parsloe 2001, p. 1). Building this tolerance for ambiguity, before, during and after interviewing clients, is a central construct in reflexive practice and is a key theme in an empathic and strengths-based approach.

Transformative learning practices

This brings us into the territory of what some term *transformative learning* and which Cranton (2002, p.64) says is 'elegantly simple'. It occurs through an event – a chance occurrence in life or in structured learning settings – where 'an individual becomes aware of holding a limiting or distorted view' and so begins to question their underlying assumptions about the world. Taylor (1998, pp. 6–7) notes that these distorted views 'support us by providing an explanation of the happenings in our daily lives but at the same time they are a reflection of our cultural and psychological assumptions' and so they are 'underpinned by sets of unquestioned assumptions about the way the world is'.

Transformative learning occurs when there is a significant change in a person's meaning structures sometimes as a result of a cumulative learning process, often as a consequence of a what Mezirow (1995) terms a 'disorientating dilemma' that leads a person to critically reflect on the assumptions that underpin their meaning structures. Such reflection may lead to recognition of discontent and the subsequent trial and adoption of a new meaning perspective incorporating new knowledge, roles, skills, values and relationships (Mezirow

1995). Some questions that may help with this process include the following:

What are some of the recurring issues, problems and insights in my interviewing practice?
What significant issues, problems or insights stand out for me?
What sort of pattern is there to my responses to these issues, problems and insights?
What evidence of changes in my knowledge, perspectives or skills have I noticed over some recent period of time?
What particular experiences or insights were these changes associated with?

The processes of reflective and transformative learning often involve changing relationships between people, based on a critical review of a range of dynamics such as power, gender and spirituality. Morrell and O'Connor (2002, p. xvii) describe these transformative learning processes as involving '… our understanding of ourselves and our self-locations; our relationships with other humans and with the natural world; our understanding of relations of power in interlocking structures of class, race and gender; our body-awareness, our vision of alternative approaches to living; and our sense of possibilities for social justice and peace and personal joy'. So reflexive learning allows existing knowledge and values to be questioned and new knowledge to be adopted based on increased self-understanding. The process is a lifelong one where new understanding can occur continuously over time, offering needed protection against professional cynicism and burnout.

Key points about reflexive learning and practice

➤ Self-appraisal and reflection are essential aspects of reflexive practice

➤ Reflexive practitioners review the currency of knowledge from professional education

➤ To the reflexive learner or practitioner, all knowledge is open to scrutiny

➤ Reflexive professionals avoid blind acceptance of previous theory and ideas

➤ Cynicism and the danger of burnout work against a reflexive approach

➤ Practitioners need mentors who are beyond the mainstream views of their professions

➤ Reflexive practice includes tolerance for ambiguity in interviewing work with clients

➤ Transformative learning develops lifelong habits of knowing, thinking and behaving.

CHAPTER OVERVIEW AND CONCLUSION

This final chapter has discussed aspects of stress and professional burnout with suggestions for how this is able to be managed with a mixture of skills, values and organizational responses that support practitioners in responding to the challenges of their emotional labour. Part of the repertoire of skills that can protect practitioners from stress and burnout is the ability to respond reflexively to the demands of professional life and this chapter has attempted to arm practitioners accordingly.

This book has travelled across a wide range of variables – through the description of contexts, stages and skills and process to empathic response types and directional skills in managing the interviews in the human service context. Other frameworks from goal and action work and motivational, cognitive-behavioural and crisis-focused approaches indicated some of the complexity of professional interviewing work in the human services. A book of this type can cover only so much, and of necessity leaves out many issues. There is always more to be learned, however, by reading, engaging and reflecting.

Epilogue

The skills and understanding that you have developed will be useful to you in your other endeavours whether this is as a student or a practitioner. I hope you appreciate that the book forms but a part of a longer and more complex process of learning and self-development. If this book has strengthened your interest in and commitment to effective reflexive practice with clients, it will sustain your further development as a professional interviewer, counsellor and communicator, both personally and professionally. The foundation supplied by this book can be built on further by strengthening existing competence, developing expertise in additional skills and by understanding theories to apply in helping clients with special needs. The complex world of professional practice is full of challenges, surprises and achievements and the most essential feature of such work is, I believe, when practitioners engage with clients in a mutual enterprise of self-discovery and solution seeking. Helping is for better or worse as mentioned previously and effective practitioners have far-reaching and positive impacts. The work of many may be undermined by cost saving pressures and further challenged by increased social dislocation and poverty. More than ever society needs empathic and competent professional helpers who, with a sense of purpose and deliberate focusing, will invest their energy in a culturally appropriate way for the benefit of their clients.

By way of a personal note, it is my sincere wish that this book has been an interesting and worthwhile experience for all those reading it and that it will assist you to manage the challenges of professional interviewing in your field of work with self-awareness and competence. This journey towards personal competence, autonomy and self-awareness is a lifelong one where there is always something new to learn – about others and about ourselves – at all stages of our lives. I like the idea that we are on a constant search for better appreciation of ourselves although we may not know the purpose of our search until we attain our own levels of deeper self-understanding. The search, like happiness, *is* the journey – both a process and an outcome – and always remains worth the commitment.

References

Aldridge, Meryl (1996) 'Dragged to Market: Being a Profession in the Postmodern World', *British Journal of Social Work*, Vol.26, pp. 177–194

Alston, Margaret and McKinnon, Jennifer (2001) *Social Work: Fields of Practice*, South Melbourne: Oxford University Press

Andrews, Donald Arthur and Bonta, James (2003) *The Psychology of Criminal Conduct*, Cincinnati: Anderson Publishing

Australian Institute of Criminology (1998) *Australian Crime; Facts & Figures 1998*, Canberra, ACT: Australian Institute of Criminology

Bankart, Peter (1997) *Talking Cures: A History of Western and Eastern Psychotherapies*, Pacific Grove CA: Brooks/Cole

Barlow, David H. [Ed.] (2001) *Clinical Handbook of Psychological Disorders: A Step-by-Step Treatment Manual*, New York: Guilford Press

Barnett, Ronald (1997) *Higher Education: A Critical Business*, Buckingham: SRHE and Open University Press

Barsky, Allan (2000) *Conflict Resolution for the Helping Professions*, Belmont: Brooks/Cole

Beck, Aaron T. (1989) *Cognitive Therapy and the Emotional Disorders*, London: Penguin

Beck, Judith S. (1995) *Cognitive Therapy: Basics and Beyond*, New York: Guilford Press

Beck, Robert (2000) *Motivation: Theory and Principles*, New Jersey: Prentice Hall

Berg, Bruce (2001) *Qualitative Research Methods for the Social Sciences*, Boston: Allyn and Bacon

Berkowitz, Leonard (2000) *Causes and Consequences of Feelings*, Studies in Emotion and Social Interaction, Cambridge UK: Cambridge University Press

Bernstein, Gail (1999) *Human Service? That Must Be So Rewarding: A Practical Guide for Professional Development*, Sydney: MacLennan-Petty

Brammer, Lawrence and MacDonald, Ginger (1999) *The Helping Relationship: Process and Skills* (7th Ed.), Boston: Allyn and Bacon

Bride, Brian; Robinson, Margaret; Yegidis, Bonnie and Figley, Charles (2003) 'Development and Validation of the Secondary Traumatic Stress Scale', *Research on Social Work Practice*, Vol.31, No.10, pp. 1–16

Brookfield, Stephen (1992) 'Developing Criteria for Formal Theory Building in Adult Education', *Adult Education Quarterly*, Vol.42, No.2, pp. 79–93

Burgoon, Judee; Buller, David and Woodall, W. Gill (1996) *Nonverbal Communication: The Unspoken Dialogue* (2nd Ed.), New York: McGraw-Hill

Buys, Nicholas and Kendall, Elizabeth (1998) 'Stress and Burnout Among Rehabilitation Counsellors Within the Context of Insurance-Based Rehabilitation: An Institutional-Level Analysis', *Journal of Rehabilitation Counselling*, Vol.4, No.1, pp. 1–12

Cameron, Helen (2003) 'Educating the Social Work Practitioner', *Australian Journal of Adult Learning*, Vol.43, No.3, pp. 361–379

Cameron, Helen (2006) 'Adult offenders' in Eric Hong Chui and Jill Wilson (Eds.) *Best Practice in the Field of Social Work and Human Services*, Sydney: Federation Press, pp. 56–82

Cameron, Helen and Telfer, Jon (2004) 'Cognitive-Behavioural Group Work: Its Application to Specific Offenders', *The Howard Journal of Criminal Justice*, Vol.43, No.1, pp. 47–64

Camilleri, Peter (1996) *Re-constructing Social Work: Exploring Social Work through Text and Talk*, Hants: Avebury

Carcach, Carlos and Grant, Anna (2000) 'Imprisonment in Australia: The Offence Composition of Australian Correctional Populations, 1998 and 1999', *Trends & Issues in Crime and Criminal Justice*, No.164, Canberra ACT: Australian Institute of Criminology

Carkhuff, Robert (1977) *The Art of Helping*, Amherst: Human Resource Development Press

Chaplin, Jocelyn (1997) 'Counselling and Gender' in Stephen Palmer and Gladeana McMahon (Eds.) *Handbook of Counselling*, (2nd Ed.), pp. 269–284, London: Routledge

Coale, Helen (1998) *The Vulnerable Therapist: Practicing Psychotherapy in an Age of Anxiety*, New York: The Haworth Press

Cooper, Joel R. (1995) 'Beware of Professional Burnout', *The Medical Reporter*, April 1st, 1995, http://medicalreporter.health.org/tmr0495/tmr2burn0495.html

Corey, Gerald; Corey, Marianne and Callanan, Patrick (2007) *Issues and Ethics in the Helping Professions*, Belmont CA: Thomson/Brooks Cole

Corey, Marianne Schneider and Corey, Gerald (1999) *Becoming a Helper* (3rd Ed.), Pacific Grove CA: Brooks/Cole

Cormier, Sherry and Nurius, Paula (2003) *Interviewing and Change Strategies for Helpers: Fundamental Skills and Cognitive Behavioral Interventions*, Pacific Grove CA: Brooks/Cole Thomson Learning

Cormier, William and Cormier, Sherry (1998) *Interviewing Strategies for Helpers: Fundamental Skills and Cognitive Behavioral Interventions*, Pacific Grove CA: Brooks/Cole

Cournoyer, Barry (2000) *The Social Work Skills Book*, Belmont: Brooks/Cole

Crain, William (1992) *Theories of Development: Concepts and Applications* (3rd Ed.), Englewood Cliffs: Prentice Hall

Cranton, Patricia (2002) 'Teaching for Transformation', *New Directions for Adult and Continuing Education*, No. 93, 63–71.

Cupach, William and Canary, David (1997) *Competence in Interpersonal Conflict*, New York: McGraw-Hill

Davis, Ann and Garrett, Paul Michael (2004) 'Progressive Practice for Tough Times: Social Work, Poverty and Division in the Twenty-First Century' in Mark Lymbery and Sandra Butler (Eds.) *Social Work Ideals and Practice Realities*, Houndmills: Palgrave Macmillan, pp. 13–33

De Jong, Peter and Berg, Insoo Kim (2008) *Interviewing for Solutions*, Pacific Grove: Brooks/Cole

Despenser, Sally (2007) 'Risk Assessment: The Personal Safety of the Counsellor', *Therapy Today*, March 2007 http://www.therapytoday.net/archive/current/index.html accessed April 2007

DiClemente, Carlo and Velasquez, Mary (2002) 'Motivational Interviewing and the Stages of Change' in William Miller and Stephen Rollnick (Eds.) *Motivational Interviewing: Preparing People for Change* (2nd Ed.), New York: The Guilford Press, pp. 201–216

Donovan, Francis and Jackson, Alun (1991) *Managing Human Service Organisations*, Sydney: Prentice Hall

Edwards, Richard; Ranson, Stewart and Strain, Michael (2002) 'Reflexivity: Towards a Theory of Lifelong Learning', *International Journal of Lifelong Education*, Vol.21, No.6, pp. 525–536

Egan, Gerard (2007) *The Skilled Helper: A Problem-Management and Opportunity-Development Approach to Helping* (8th Ed.), Belmont: Thomson Brooks/Cole

Ellis, Albert (1998) *Rational Emotive Behavior Therapy: A Therapist's Guide*, San Jose CA: Impact

Erdman, David V. (Ed.) (1992) *The Complete Poetry and Prose of William Blake*, New York: Anchor

Festinger, Leon (1957) *A Theory of Cognitive Dissonance*, Stanford: Stanford University Press

Fook, Jan (1999) 'Critical Reflectivity in Education and Practice' in Bob Pease and Jan Fook (Ed.) *Transforming Social Work Practice: Postmodern Critical Perspectives*, Studies in Society Series, St. Leonards: Allen and Unwin, pp. 195–208

Freidson, Eliot (1986) *Professional Powers*, Chicago: University of Chicago Press

Gaveaux, Dominique (2006) 'Crowd or Bonus', *Therapy Today*, July 2006 http://www.therapytoday.net/archive/current/index.html accessed April 2007

Geldard, David (1999) *Basic Personal Counselling: A Training Manual for Counsellors*, Sydney: Prentice Hall

Giddens, Anthony (1991) *Modernity and Self-identity: Self and Society in the Late Modern Age*, Cambridge: Polity

Gorkin, Mark (2005) 'Does Your Organization Practice Safe Stress? Seven Intervention Strategies' The Stress Doc, http://www.stressdoc.com/organizational_safe_stress.html accessed May 2005

Greenberg, Jerrold (1997) *Comprehensive Stress Management*, Madison: Brown and Benchmark

Griffin, Emory (1994) *A First Look at Communication Theory*, New York: McGraw Hill

Gudykunst, William B. and Kim, Young Yun (1997) *Communicating with Strangers: An Approach to Intercultural Communication* (3rd Ed.), New York: McGraw-Hill

Harrison, W. David (1991) *Seeking Common Ground: A Theory of Social Work in Social Care*, Hants: Avebury

Hogg, Russell and Brown, David (1998) *Rethinking Law & Order*, Annandale, NSW: Pluto Press

Holmes, Ronald and Holmes, Stephen (2005) *Suicide: Theory, Practice and Investigation*, Thousand Oaks: Sage Publications

Howe, David (1994), 'Modernity, Postmodernity and Social Work', *British Journal of Social Work*, No.24, pp. 513–532.

Hugman, Richard (2005) *New Approaches in Ethics for the Caring Professions*, Houndsmill: Palgrave Macmillan

Hunt, Alan (1999) *Governing Morals: A Social History of Moral Regulation*, Melbourne: Cambridge University Press

Hutchins, David E. and Vaught, Claire Cole (1997) *Helping Relationships and Strategies* (3rd Ed.), Pacific Grove: Brooks/Cole

Ivey, Allen E. and Ivey, Mary Bradford (2003) *Intentional Interviewing and Counselling: Facilitating Client Development in a Multicultural Society* (5th Ed.), Pacific Grove: Thomson Brooks/Cole

Ivey, Allen E. and Ivey, Mary Bradford (2008) *Essentials of Intentional Interviewing: Counselling in a Multicultural World*, Belmont CA: Thomson Brooks/Cole

Jackson, Alun and Donovan, Francis (1999) *Managing to Survive: Managerial Practice in Not-for-profit Organisations*, St. Leonards: Allen and Unwin

James, Richard and Gilliland, Burl (2001) *Crisis Intervention Strategies* (4th Ed.), Belmont CA: Wadsworth/Thompson Learning

Jamrozik, Adam (2005) *Social Policy in the Post-Welfare State: Australian Society in the 21st Century* (2nd Ed.), Frenchs Forest: Pearson Education Australia

Johnson, David (1997) *Reaching Out: Interpersonal Effectiveness and Self Actualization*, New York: Allyn and Bacon

Johnson, Terence (1972) *Professions and Power*, London: The Macmillan Press

Jones, Andrew and May, John (1992) *Working in Human Service Organisations: A Critical Introduction*, Melbourne: Longman Cheshire

Kadushin, Alfred and Kadushin, Goldie (1997) *The Social Work Interview: A Guide for Human Service Professionals* (4th Ed.), New York: Columbia University Press

Kottler, Jeffrey (2000) *Doing Good: Passion and Commitment for Helping Others*, Philadelphia: Brunner-Routledge

Krahn, Gloria L.; Thom, V. A.; Hale, B. J. and Williams, K. (1995) 'Running on Empty: A Look at Burnout in Early Intervention Professionals', *Infants and Young Children*, Vol.7, No.4, pp. 1–11

Kubler-Ross, Elisabeth (1970) *On Death and Dying*, London: Tavistock

Kvale, Steinar (1989) 'To Validate is to Question' in Steinar Kvale, (Ed.) *Issues of Validity in Qualitative Research*, Lund: Studentlitteratur, pp. 73–92

Kvale, Steinar (1996) *Interviews: An Introduction to Qualitative Research Interviewing*, Thousand Oaks: Sage Publications

Lazarus, Richard S. (1991) *Emotion and Adaptation*, Oxford: Oxford University Press.

Lazarus, Richard S. (2001) 'Relational Meaning and Discrete Emotions' in K. R. Scherer, A. Schorr and T. Johnstone (Eds.) *Appraisal Processes in Emotion*, Oxford: Oxford University Press, pp. 121–140.

Legge, K. (1995), *Human Resource Management: Rhetorics & Realities*, London: MacMillan Business

Levinson, David (1994) *Aggression and Conflict: A Cross-Cultural Encyclopedia*, California: ABC-CLIO Inc.

Luxemburg, Rosa (1951) *The Accumulation of Capital*, Translated from the German by Agnes Schwarzschild, London: Routledge and Kegan Paul

MacDonald, David and Brown, Melanie (1996) 'Indicators of Aggressive Behaviour', *Research & Public Policy Series*, Canberra ACT: Australian Institute of Criminology

Mahoney, Michael J. (1974) *Cognition and Behavior Modification*, Cambridge, MA: Ballinger.

Maslach, Christina and Leiter, P. Michael (1999) 'Take this Job and ... Love It! 6 Ways to Beat Burnout', *Psychology Today*, September/October 1999, pp. 50–53

Matthews, Judith and Candy, Philip (1999) 'New Dimensions in the Dynamics of Learning and Knowledge' in David Boud and John Garrick (Eds.) *Understanding Learning at Work*, London: Routledge, pp. 47–64

McLaren, Helen (2007) 'Exploring the Ethics of Forewarning: Social Workers, Confidentially and Potential Child Abuse Disclosures', *Ethics and Social Welfare*, Vol.1, No.1, pp. 22–40

McGuire, James (2000 a) 'Defining Correctional Programs', *What Works in Corrections* Vol.12, No.2 [online]:http://www.csc-scc.gc.ca/text/pblct/ forum/e122/ e122a_e.html accessed March 2005

McGuire, James (2000 b) *Cognitive-Behavioural Approaches: An Introduction to Theory and Research*, Online Only: http://www.homeoffice.gov.uk/docs/cogbeh.pdf accessed April 2005

McGuire, James (2004) *Understanding Psychology and Crime*, Berkshire: Open University Press/McGraw Hill Education

Meichenbaum, Donald (1995) 'Cognitive-Behavioral Therapy in Historical Perspective', in B. Bongar and L. E. Beutler (Eds.) *Comprehensive Textbook of Psychotherapy: Theory and Practice*, New York: Oxford University Press, pp. 140–158

Mezirow, Jack (1995) 'Transformation Theory of Adult Learning' in M. Welton (Ed.) *In Defense of the Lifeworld*, New York: SUNY Press, pp. 39–70.

Micsek, K.; Haney, M.; Tidey, J.; Vivian J. and Weerts, E. (1994) 'Neurochemistry and Pharmacotherapeutic Management of Aggression and Violence' in Albert Reiss and Jeffrey Roth (Eds.) *Understanding and Preventing Violence, Volume 2*, Washington: National Academy Press, pp. 245–514

Miller, William R. and Rollnick, Stephen (1991) *Motivational Interviewing: Preparing People to Change Addictive Behavior*, New York: The Guildford Press

Miller, William R. and Rollnick, Stephen (2002) *Motivational Interviewing: Preparing People for Change* (2nd Ed.), New York: The Guilford Press

Mindframe (2006) *Reporting Suicide and Mental Illness: A Mindframe Resource for Media Professionals*, www.mindframe-media.info accessed April 2006

Moir, A. and Moir, B. (1998) 'Sense & Sensitivity: A Review of Why Men Don't Iron: The Real Science of Gender', *The Weekend Australian*, October 17–18.

Morrell, Amish and O'Connor, Mary (2002) 'Introduction' in E. O'Sullivan, A. Morrell and M. O'Connor (Eds.) *Expanding the Boundaries of Transformative Learning: Essays on Theory and Praxis*, New York: Palgrave, pp. xv–xx

Mukherjee, Satyanshu; Carcach, Carlos and Higgins, Karl (1997) *A Statistical Profile of Crime in Australia*, Research & Public Policy Series, Canberra. ACT: Australian Institute of Criminology

Myers, David (1993) *Social Psychology*, New York: McGraw-Hill

Nelson-Jones, Richard (1997) *Practical Counselling and Helping Skills: Text and Exercises for the Life Skills Counselling Model* (4th Ed.), London: Cassell

Neukrug, Edward (2004) *Theory, Practice and Trends in Human Services: An Introduction*, Pacific Grove: Brooks/Cole-Thomson Learning

O'Connor, Ian; Wilson, Jill and Setterlund, Deborah (1998) *Social Work and Welfare Practice*, Melbourne: Longman

Okun, Barbara and Kantrowitz, Ricki (2008) *Effective Helping: Interviewing and Counselling Techniques*, Belmont, CA: Thomson Brooks/Cole

Pareek, Udai and Rao, T. Venkateswara (1980) 'Cross-cultural Surveys and Interviewing' in H. C. Triandis and W. L. Berry (Eds.) *Handbook of Cross-cultural Psychology, Vol. 2 Methodology*, Boston: Allyn and Bacon, pp. 127–179

Parsloe, Phyllida (2001) 'Looking Back on Social Work Education', *Social Work Education*, Vol.20, No.1, pp. 9–19

Pearson, Judy Cornelia; West, Richard and Turner, Lynn (1995) *Gender and Communication* (3rd Ed.), Boston: McGraw-Hill

Pines, Ayala; Ben-Ari, Adital; Utasi, Agnes and Larson, Dale (2002) 'A Cross-cultural Investigation of Social Support and Burnout', *European Psychologist*, Vol.7, No.4, pp. 256–264

Potter, Jonathon (1996) 'Attitudes, Social Representations and Discursive Psychology', in Margaret Wetherell (Ed.) *Identities, Groups and Social Issues,* London: Sage Publications, pp. 119–174

Reeves, Andrew and Nelson, Sue (2006) 'Tight Ropes and Safety Nets', *Therapy Today*, February 2006, http://www.therapytoday.net/archive/current/index.html accessed April 2007

Rogers, Carl R. (1951) *Client-Centered Therapy*, Boston: Houghton Mifflin

Rose, Nikolas (1998) *Inventing Our Selves: Psychology, Power and Personhood*, New York: Cambridge University Press

Sacco, Terry (1996) 'Towards an Inclusive Paradigm for Social Work' in Mark Doel and Steven Shardlow (Eds.) *Social Work in a Changing World: An International Perspective on Practice Learning*, Aldershot, England: Arena /Ashgate, pp. 31–42

Saleebey, Dennis (1994) 'Culture, Theory and Narrative: The Intersection of Meanings in Practice', *Social Work*, No.39, pp. 351–359

Saleebey, Dennis (1997) *The Strengths Perspective in Social Work Practice* (2nd Ed.), New York: Longman

Scherwitz, L. and Rugulies, R. (1992) 'Life-Style and Hostility' in Howard Friedman (Ed.) *Hostility, Coping & Health*, Washington: American Psychological Association, pp. 77–98

Schön, Donald (1991) *Educating the Reflective Practitioner: Towards a New Design for Teaching and Learning in the Professions*, Oxford: Jossey–Bass

Shelden, Randall (2001) *Controlling the Dangerous Classes: A Critical Introduction to the History of Criminal Justice*, Needham Heights, MA: Allyn and Bacon

Simos, Gregoris (Ed.) (2002) *Cognitive Behaviour Therapy: A Guide for the Practicing Clinician*, East Sussex; Brunner-Routledge:

Singer, Peter (1994) *Ethics*, Oxford: Oxford University Press

Stacks, Don W.; Hill, Sidney R. Jr. and Hickson, Mack III (1991) *An Introduction to Communication Theory*, Fort Worth: Holt, Rinehart and Winston

Stewart, Charles and Cash, William (2003) *Interviewing Principles and Practice*, Boston: McGraw Hill

Swain, Phillip (2002) 'Confidentiality, Record Keeping and Practice' in Phillip Swain (Ed.) *In the Shadow of the Law: The Legal Context of Social Work Practice*, Annandale: Federation Press, pp. 28–49

Swan, Norman (1998) 'Mastering the Control Factor, Part One', *The Health Report*, ABC Radio National, http://www.abc.net.au/rn/talks/8.30/helthrpt/stories/s14314.htm accessed Nov 2004.

Taylor, Carolyn and White, Susan (2000) *Practising Reflexivity in Health and Welfare*, Buckingham: Open University Press

Timmins, C. L. (2002) 'The Impact of Language Barriers on the Health Care of Latinos in the United States: A Review of the Literature and Guidelines for Practice', *Journal of Midwifery and Women's Health*, Vol.47, pp. 80–96

Usher, Robin; Bryant, Ian and Johnston, Rennie (1997) *Adult Education and the Postmodern Challenge: Learning Beyond the Limits*, London: Routledge

Wagner, Christopher and Sanchez, Francisco (2002) 'The Role of Values in Motivational Interviewing' in William Miller and Stephen Rollnick (Eds.) *Motivational Interviewing: Preparing People for Change* (2nd Ed.), New York: The Guilford Press, pp. 284–298

Walker, Alison; Kershaw, Chris and Nicholas, Sian (2006) *Crime in England and Wales 2005/2006*, National Statistics, UK: Home Office

Westra, Matthew (1996) *Active Communication*, Pacific Grove: Brooks/Cole

Whitehead, Anna; Ryba, Ken and O'Driscoll, Michael (2000) 'Burnout Among New Zealand Primary School Teachers', *New Zealand Journal of Psychology*, Vol.29, No.2, pp. 51–60

Willcox, Linda (2006) 'When the Client Signs', *Therapy Today*, December 2006 http://www.therapytoday.net/archive/current/index.html accessed April 2007

Wilmot, William and Hocker, Joyce (2001) *Interpersonal Conflict* (5th Ed.), Boston: McGraw-Hill

Winter, Ian (Ed.) (2000) *Social Capital and Public Policy in Australia*, Melbourne: Australian Institute of Family Studies

Woolfolk, Robert (1998) *The Cure of Souls: Science, Values and Psychotherapy*, San Francisco: Jossey-Bass

Young, Mark (1998) *Learning the Art of Helping: Building Blocks and Techniques*, Upper Saddle River: Merrill Prentice Hall

Index